ANTONELLO DA MESSINA

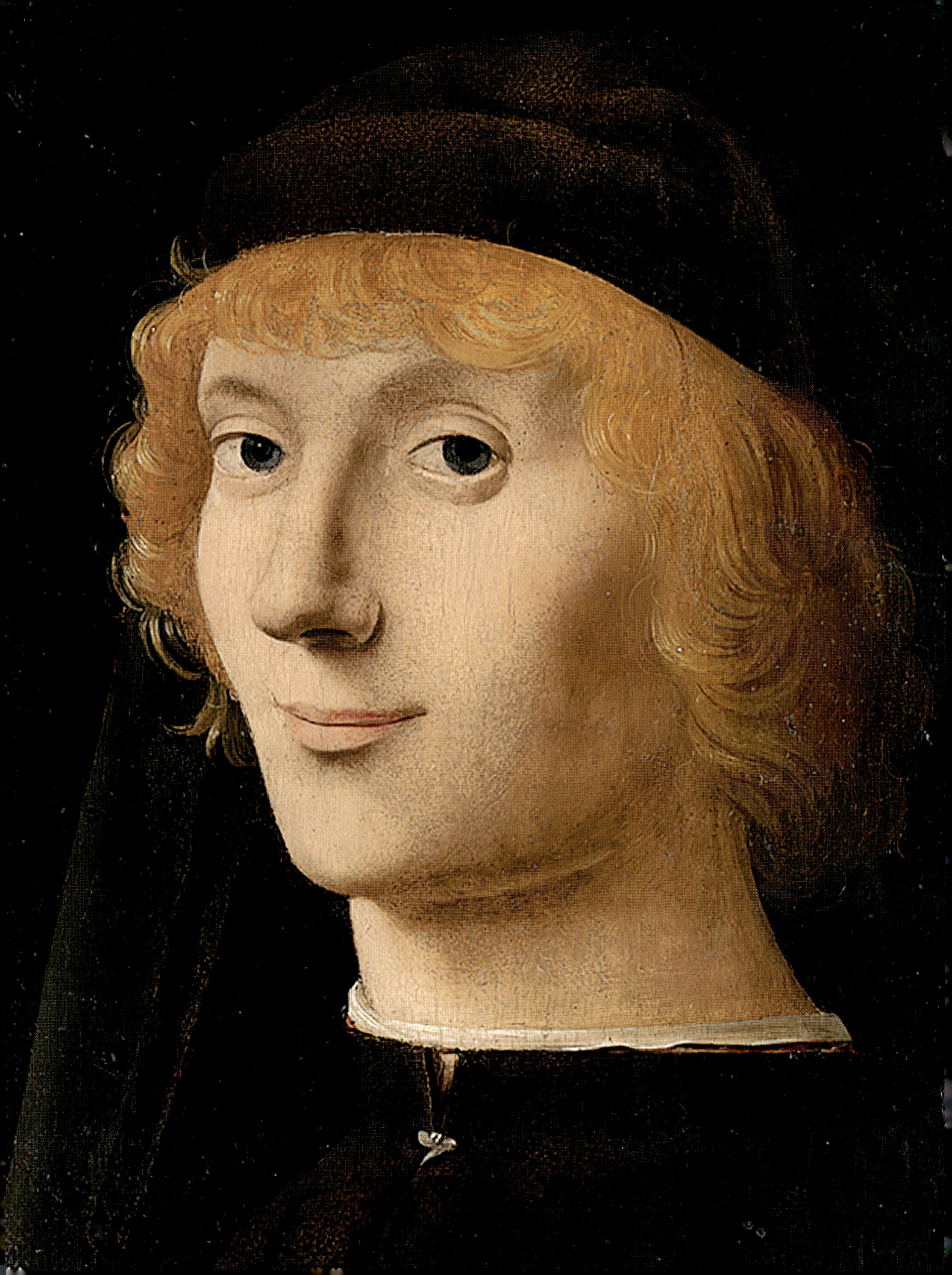

ANTONELLO DA MESSINA

Sicily's Renaissance Master

GIOACCHINO BARBERA

with contributions by

Keith Christiansen and Andrea Bayer

The Metropolitan Museum of Art, New York

Yale University Press, New Haven and London

This volume has been published in conjunction with the exhibition "Antonello da Messina: Sicily's Renaissance Master" held at The Metropolitan Museum of Art, New York, December 13, 2005–March 5, 2006

The exhibition was organized and made possible by the Cultural Commissioner for the Sicilian Region, Hon. Alessandro Pagano, and the Foundation for Italian Art and Culture, with the generous support of Bulgari and ACP Group.

Additional support has been provided by the Gail and Parker Gilbert Fund and the Italian Cultural Institute of New York.

This exhibition catalogue is made possible by the Drue E. Heinz Fund.

Published by The Metropolitan Museum of Art, New York

Second printing, 2006

John P. O'Neill, Editor in Chief
Gwen Roginsky, Associate General Manager of Publications
Ellen Shultz, Editor
Bruce Campbell, Designer
Margaret Rennolds Chace, Managing Editor
Peter Antony, Chief Production Manager
Sally Van Devanter, Production Manager
Robert Weisberg, Assistant Managing Editor
Jean Wagner, Bibliographer

The essay and three entries by Gioacchino Barbera translated from the Italian by Lawrence Jenkens

Library of Congress Cataloging-in-Publication Data
Barbera, Gioacchino.
Antonello da Messina : Sicily's Renaissance master / Gioacchino Barbera, with contributions by Keith Christiansen and Andrea Bayer.
p. cm.
Catalog of an exhibition to be held at the Metropolitan Museum of Art, New York, Dec. 13, 2005–Mar. 5, 2006.
Includes bibliographical references.
ISBN 1-58839-177-9 (pbk.) -- ISBN 0-300-11648-9 (Yale University Press)
1. Antonello, da Messina, 1430?–1479—Exhibitions. I. Antonello, da Messina, 1430?–1479. II. Christiansen, Keith. III. Bayer, Andrea.
IV. Metropolitan Museum of Art (New York, N.Y.) V. Title.
ND623.A53952A4 2005
759.5—dc22

2005030041

Cover: *The Virgin Annunciate* (cat. 6)
Frontispiece: *Portrait of a Man* (cat. 5)

Printed and bound in Italy

Contents

Statement by the Cultural Commissioner for the Sicilian Region

As a modern citizen of Sicily I take pride in presenting these works by Antonello da Messina, one of the greatest Sicilians and one of the foremost artists of all time. He was born in a town on the periphery of the Kingdom of the Two Sicilies at the end of the Middle Ages, and yet he attained a place for himself on the larger stage of international culture; indeed, he reached its apogee, and became a source of inspiration for other artists. In describing his San Cassiano altarpiece (fig. 3), the erudite humanist Matteo Colazio, writing from Venice, named "Antonellum siculum" (Antonello of Sicily) as the one painter alive capable of imitating the perfection of the art of antiquity. He was praised in the same humanist circles for his ability to create figures "so well that they seemed alive and missing only a soul" (Marin Sanudo) since he "made inanimate things seem real and animate creatures seem alive" (F. Maurolico).

Antonello was an outstanding artist, whose works embodied the great cultural traditions of Renaissance Europe. His paintings, executed in Sicily, Naples, and Venice, combine a Netherlandish interest in minute descriptive detail, a Provençal tendency toward stylization of the figure, the emotional timber of Giovanni Bellini's Venetian colorism, and Piero della Francesca's synthesis of spatial representation and perspective. These are the principal cultural threads woven together in the art of the age of humanism and the Renaissance. Antonello possessed an extraordinary ability to synthesize and simplify figures and objects into pure geometry, and they are brought to life by the quality of the light that caresses their surfaces, giving them clarity and depth, and, in the case of the sitters, psychological presence. In his paintings, it is the color in addition to the carefully modulated light that lends substance to the forms and defines their planes.

Antonello's portraits are extraordinary (especially in comparison to the prevailing contemporary profile portraits) for their inventiveness and for their almost "photographic" realism, underscored by the subtle positioning of the sitter in space. The lesson we glean from Antonello's portrait studies, so often evocative although their subjects remain anonymous, like the one long referred to as the "Unknown Sailor" (cat. 3) in Cefalù, is of the terrible disadvantage that the loss of identity poses. We no longer can attach a name to the sitter and, worse still, cannot even speculate about whom and what he might have been. This is emblematic, too, of the urgent cultural problems we currently face as a result of the homogenizing process of globalization. Antonello's work points to the importance of recovering traditions and the fundamental values underlying them as a basis for our own future. Thus, we have allocated government resources at the ministry of Beni Culturali in Sicily toward furthering the concept of "Identity and the Future," even when the work in question belongs to the "Patrimony of Humanity."

Antonello's art reflects most authentically and in the deepest sense that "being Sicilian" means being a citizen of the world. The atmosphere in his paintings, whether portraits or images of saints or of the Madonna, always invokes Sicily. As the author Leonardo Sciascia, another great Sicilian, defined it, "man['s] life and his vision of his life are irrevocably conditioned by the places and the people among whom . . . [he] is born and is raised and reaches adulthood." Also Sicilian, metaphorically, was Antonello's ability to achieve success even though he began life at a disadvantage. Like all southerners, Antonello was also an "emigrant"; in the course of his travels he would learn a great deal while also disseminating his style throughout Europe. Today, his work can be found in the most important art museums worldwide.

A poignant feature of Antonello's images of the Madonna, beginning with the *Virgin Annunciate* (cat. 6) in the Palazzo Abatellis, is that they convey the innocence and purity of Southern Italian women—a natural beauty that we call "*acqua e sapone*" (soap and water). The outdoor settings of his paintings of the Crucifixion capture the vastness of the Sicilian countryside and the distant Straits of Messina; these are actual landscapes still recognizable today, and the spirit of the figures that inhabit them will never be diminished.

The *Virgin Annunciate* confronts us with the gentle but startled gesture of an educated young woman who has been surprised by the appearance of an unexpected visitor, bearing a curious message, having arrived suddenly with the lightness of a breath of wind and the brilliance of a ray of sunshine. The reservation visible in her pose and in the solemn gesture of her small hand betrays the intimacy of her silent acknowledgment of the mysterious news she has just received. The contents of the message are translated in profoundly human terms and we comprehend its significance personally. The story of the Virgin is thus told without words, her acceptance of her fate hidden behind her glance, but the eyes of the angel tell all.

Alessandro Pagano
Cultural Commissioner for the Sicilian Region

Letter from the Chairman, Foundation for Italian Art and Culture

It is impossible to think of Antonello da Messina's unique artistry and virtuosity without considering the city and island of his birth. He was, in many respects, the paradigmatic figure of Sicilian culture: someone who profited from the island's strategic position in the Mediterranean and its vast commercial ties with Northern as well as Southern Europe—with the Netherlands as well as with France, Spain, and the Italian peninsula. Whether Antonello actually journeyed to the Netherlands or Southern France for his training has long been debated. He certainly spent time in Naples and by 1475 had arrived in Venice, where his presence was to transform the artistic landscape. In the truest sense he was an international figure, and the style he created may be seen as European—a highly personal synthesis of the greatest achievements of the Renaissance north and south of the Alps. In his art the descriptive world of Jan van Eyck and Petrus Christus meets the elevated, perspectival vision of Piero della Francesca.

Homer called Sicily the Island of the Sun and his greatest hero, Ulysses, performed on the slopes of Mount Etna one of his most famous feats of ingenuity. Plato traveled to the island to learn from the Pythagoreans. The philosopher Empedocles flourished on its shores. Sicilian and Greek architects built in Agrigento the only remaining unreconstructed Greek temples. From the beginning of recorded history the island provided a constant flow of artistic, scientific, and cultural excellence. Civilizations—Phoenician, Greek, Byzantine, Arab, Norman—met in Sicily and each left a rich legacy. When traveling through Sicily and viewing its artistic landmarks one is exposed to a synopsis of the art history of the West.

It is for this reason that the Foundation for Italian Art and Culture is particularly proud to bring to the United States and its foremost museum three major works by Antonello da Messina, Sicily's Renaissance master. These works are seen here for the very first time on the American continent. A larger exhibition of this artist's work, comprising loans from around the world, will open in Rome in the spring of 2006. However, Antonello's extant works are not many, and those conserved on his native island are among the best.

My thanks go to the Honorable Alessandro Pagano, the enthusiastic Cultural Commissioner for the Sicilian Region, and to the Director of the Metropolitan Museum, Philippe de Montebello. Our President, Alain Elkann, was instrumental in initiating the project. Keith Christiansen and Andrea Bayer, curators at the Metropolitan Museum, and Gioacchino Barbera and Vincenzo Abbate, Directors, respectively, of the Messina and Palermo museums that are lending Antonello's treasures from their collections, were involved in a friendly and productive collaboration. Not least, our Director, Manfredi Piccolomini, and the Foundation staff worked tirelessly to get the project off the ground.

Daniele Bodini
Chairman, Foundation for Italian Art and Culture

Director's Foreword

Some years back I was asked to name my favorite painting. It's a silly game, since any choice this subjective is bound to change with one's mood and interests at a given moment. At the time, however, a single image rose up in my mind: the *Crucifixion* by Antonello da Messina in Antwerp (fig. 4), with its sublime serenity and tonal perfection, despite its tragic subject. When, a few years later, I toured Sicily with my wife, I added to my short list of greatest paintings the unforgettable *Virgin Annunciate*. Therefore, when the loan to the Metropolitan of this and two other paintings by Antonello, now in museums in Messina and Cefalù, was proposed, I embraced the idea enthusiastically.

Antonello da Messina has always held a special—almost unique—place in the brilliant panoply of stars that make up the artistic firmament of the Italian Quattrocento. Born in the bustling but artistically undistinguished Sicilian city of Messina about the beginning of the fourth decade of the fifteenth century, he seized the opportunity to study in Naples, the most vibrant center in Southern Italy. Hints of what were probably quite extensive travels have come down to us in documents, as when we learn that the artist returned along with his family (suggesting that the trip had been of some duration) from the mainland to Messina in January 1460. Although we are unsure precisely where his travels took him, it is clear that he had a tremendous capacity to absorb the innovations of the great artists whose works he encountered, from the Netherlandish and Provençal painters so well known in Southern Italy to his Northern Italian contemporaries. From these encounters and his own formidable talent he was able to form his unrivaled and influential mature style.

By late 1474, when Antonello arrived for a long stay in Venice, local artists looked to him as an absolute leader in the design of altarpieces and as a portraitist. In both of these areas, as well as in that of small-scale devotional painting, his work was seen as so exceptional that the duke of Milan unsuccessfully tried to cajole him away from Venice, while his Venetian patron, Pietro Bon, held on to him tenaciously. Bon was adamant that the altarpiece the artist had undertaken for him, "one of the most excellent painted works either in or outside of Italy," must be completed. Despite the competition for him across Northern Italy, he returned to Messina, where he may have painted the *Virgin Annunciate* (cat. 6), one of the single finest panels of the entire century.

It is with the greatest pleasure and honor that we have accepted the offer by the Cultural Commissioner for the Sicilian Region, the Honorable Alessandro Pagano, and the Chairman of the Foundation for Italian Art and Culture, Daniele Bodini, to exhibit three masterpieces by Antonello from Sicily at the Metropolitan Museum, where they will be joined by three works by the artist (including a rare drawing attributed to him) from the Museum's collection, and another early devotional panel from a private collection. We are grateful to the Wildenstein gallery for arranging this last loan. We thank Manfredi Piccolomini and Alvise Casellati of the Foundation for Italian Art and Culture for their efforts to bring the show to New York, and the directors of the three lending institutions in Sicily, Gioacchino Barbera, Vincenzo Abbate, and Giuseppe Simplicio, who collaborated with Metropolitan curators Keith Christiansen and Andrea Bayer. Additional support has been provided by the Gail and Parker Gilbert Fund, and the Italian Cultural Institute of New York has supported both the exhibition and the public programs that will accompany it. The publication of the catalogue has been made possible by the Drue E. Heinz Fund.

Philippe de Montebello
Director, The Metropolitan Museum of Art

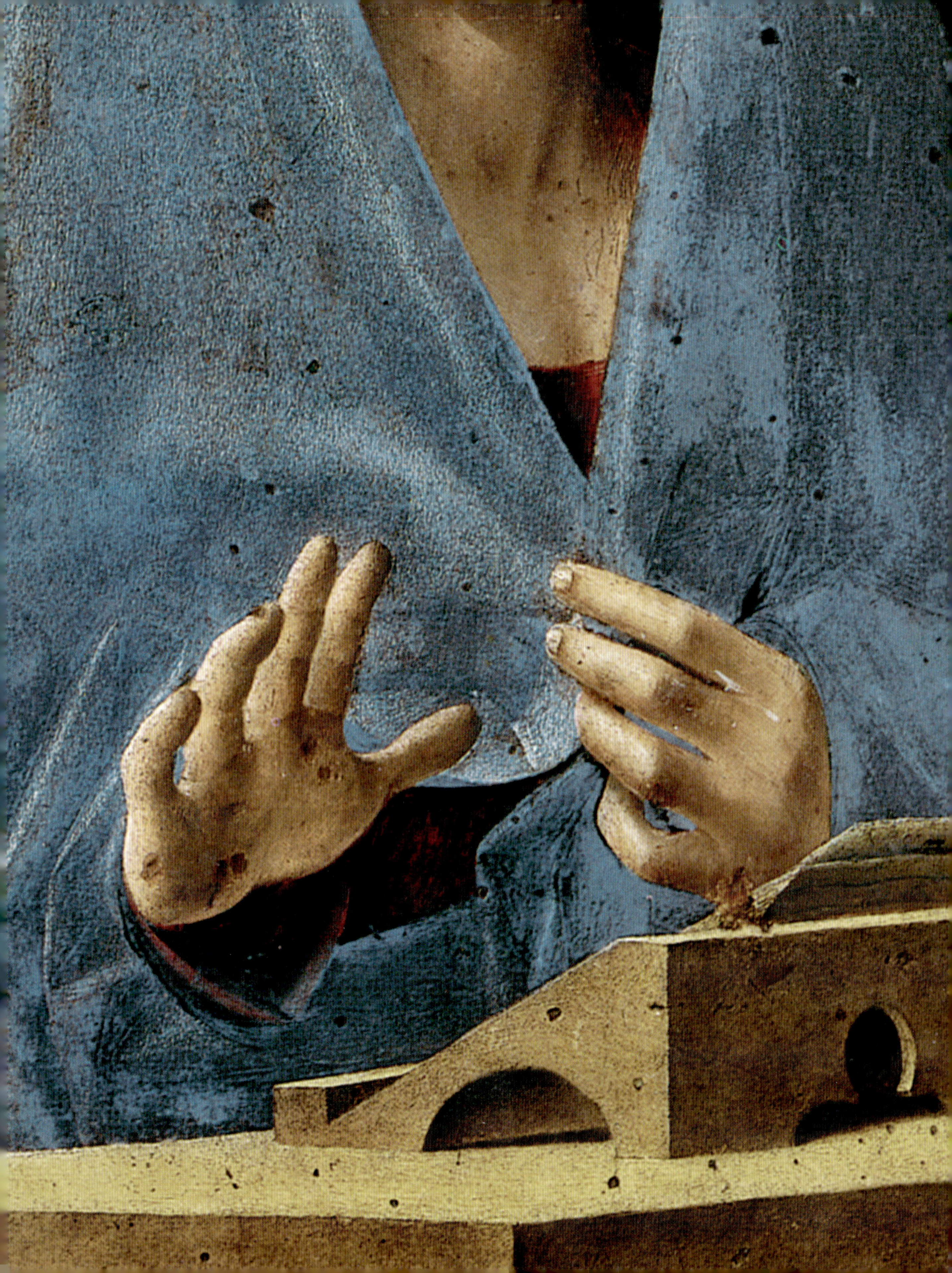

THE EXALTED ART OF ANTONELLO DA MESSINA

(about 1430–1479)

Keith Christiansen

Is it possible to do justice to one of the geniuses of the Italian Renaissance—for that is what Antonello da Messina is—with just six small panel paintings? The short answer is "no." Antonello's achievement was too varied and raises too many issues crucial to our understanding of European art. He is, in a sense, the first truly European painter. No other Italian artist of the fifteenth century responded in such a direct fashion not only to the leading masters of Bruges and Brussels—Jan van Eyck (d. 1441) and Petrus Christus (d. 1475/76) in particular—but also to those giants of French Provençal painting whose names have been painstakingly recovered through archival research and the impeccable connoisseurship of scholars such as Charles Sterling. I mean the astonishing Master of the Aix Annunciation—named after his great altarpiece of the *Annunciation* (about 1443–44) in the Église de La Madeleine in Aix-en-Provence: a master who can, with a high degree of probability, now be identified with the transplanted Northerner Barthélemy d'Eyck (documented in Provence 1444–70; whether he was a distant relation of Jan van Eyck remains speculative) and who was also responsible for the magical illustrations in an allegory of courtly love, *Le Coeur d'amour épris,* composed by his art-loving patron King René of Anjou. No less important was Enguerrand Quarton (documented in Provence 1444–66), whose *Coronation of the Virgin* (1454; Musée, Villeneuve-lès-Avignon) is one of the landmarks of French painting, and is as notable for the topographical landscape along the bottom of the picture as for the heavenly vision above. Did Antonello personally encounter any of these artists, possibly in the course of undocumented trips north of the Alps, or did he only come into contact with their work during the time he spent in Naples, where Netherlandish painting was highly valued and where, between 1438 and 1442, René of Anjou briefly ruled as King of Naples and of Sicily? Whatever the case, Antonello's achievement as a painter of portraits and landscapes is inconceivable without these great masters, and it is one of the intriguing mysteries of Italian art that the person who best understood the work of his Northern contemporaries—both Netherlandish and Franco-Flemish—was born, trained, and apparently worked for most of his career on the periphery of Europe. Obviously, much more than wine, olive oil, textiles, and other commodities was passing through the port of Messina, which in the mid-fifteenth century was experiencing an economic recession dominated by foreigners.

To artists working in a seaport, long-distance travel did not present the same difficulties it did to the more landlocked, and the question facing anyone trying to "explain" the amazing trajectory of Antonello's career is how much and where his travels may have taken him (Naples and Venice are the only destinations we are certain of). His artistic progression is truly breathtaking and transports us from the backwater of Hispano-Netherlandish devotional paintings, with their hard, linear effect, awkward draftsmanship, and heavily tooled, flat gold backgrounds, to some of the most cosmopolitan and exquisite examples of naturalistic description in European art, predicated on a complete mastery of the technique of oil painting (the aspect of Antonello's art to which Vasari attached such overriding importance,

Opposite: detail of catalogue 6

wrongly making him responsible for its introduction into Italy). His mature paintings convey as no one else's the brilliant light of Sicily, either depicted *en plein air* or filtered through the windows of those somber but elegant Sicilian palaces, constructed of the local warm brown stone that every visitor to the island remembers. His miraculous painting of Saint Jerome in his study (fig. 1) seemed to contemporaries in Venice to equal the subtle, descriptive effects of those marvels of Netherlandish art: painting as a microcosm. Indeed, the sixteenth-century Venetian connoisseur Marcantonio Michiel could not believe it was painted by an Italian, and suggested either van Eyck or Memling as a more probable attribution. The truth is that Antonello's picture possesses a harmony and geometric clarity of structure that even Jan van Eyck could not match, and the figure is scaled to the building he inhabits. It is a work first and foremost about space and light and only secondarily about the scholar-saint sitting in his well-carpentered library enclosure. The light illuminating the foreground enters the picture from the viewer's space, while the recesses of the palace are lit from windows along the back wall. Although the square windows of the ground floor offer enchanting views onto the Sicilian landscape, the Gothic biforate windows of the upper story look out onto a crystalline azure sky dotted with swallows. Typically, the palace façade with an open arch not only frames the interior view but provides the occasion for a ravishing genre scene of a partridge and a peacock and a brass bowl with water. No less memorable is Antonello's *Crucifixion* now in Antwerp (fig. 4), in which the affective figure group in the foreground is set against a landscape punctuated by city walls, a castle, and gently sloping hills leading the eye to a distant sunlit bay that yields nothing to the poetry of Seurat's views of Gravelines painted more than four centuries later. Indeed, so perfectly pitched is the sense of tone, light, and geometry that one would like to think that the nineteenth-century Frenchman knew this painting, which entered the museum in 1840.

That Antonello was a key figure in the history of Venetian painting has long been acknowledged, although his impact extended far beyond the much repeated assertion—false, as it turns out—that it was he who introduced Giovanni Bellini to the practice of oil painting (Bellini's oil is more viscous and his technique is not directly tied to either Antonello's or to Netherlandish practice). Antonello is documented in the city in 1475–76, but his visits may have been more frequent than the sparse documentation we have in hand suggests. How, given the scarcity of the evidence, do we trace the obviously enriching effects of the give-and-take between Antonello and Bellini? That Bellini's notion of portraiture was transformed by the example of the Sicilian seems probable, but was Antonello, indeed, the creator of those grand, spacious altarpieces in which the Virgin and her attendants are shown enthroned in a fictive architectural chapel designed to illusionistically extend the real space of the church, as often claimed? Whatever the case—and, unfortunately, of Antonello's landmark contribution to this genre, the San Cassiano altarpiece, of 1475–76, only fragments survive (fig. 3)—we may ponder whether any earlier artist observed and recorded the luxuriant self-absorption of Venetian life with greater acuity and wonder. Who else would have thought of adding as a backdrop to the noble, still, nude form of Saint Sebastian (fig. 2) a view of elegant Venetian palaces bordering a canal or lagoon, populated by richly dressed figures disturbingly unconcerned with the fate of the arrow-pierced youth, his head turned heavenward with a mixture of expectation and resignation? A soldier has set his halberd aside and is shown sprawled, feetfirst, asleep on the marble-paved piazza, his steeply foreshortened pose—like the setting, clearly inspired by the work of Andrea Mantegna in nearby Padua—reminding us that Antonello was acutely aware of the prestige that attached to those indications of the mastery of perspective that, as Raphael's father declared, "fooled the eye and are the glory of art." And where, we might ask, did he derive that quality of aloof detachment and sublime geometric abstraction that have called to mind for countless viewers the work of Piero della Francesca? Did the two artists meet? Did Antonello have the occasion to study Piero's work? Or are we merely dealing with kindred sensibilities fueled by access to similar theoretical, literary, and artistic sources?

These are among the intriguing issues Antonello's art poses to anyone wishing to move beyond its ravishingly complex beauties. In his essay to this catalogue, Gioacchino Barbera attempts to reconstruct the narrative of Antonello's life, but we must remember that the artist's career is no less remarkable for the lapses in documentation than it is for the quality of the paintings he produced. It could not be and is not the intention of this small exhibition to present the artist in all his complexity. Rather, the exhibition puts before the public six paintings that not only attest to the artist's stature and genius but also hint at his assimilation of the achievement of Netherlandish and Provençal painting. It does eloquent justice to his status as a supremely gifted and original portraitist: he was the first to suggest, by those unforgettable smiles that seem on the verge of breaking across and softening the often coarse faces of his male sitters (few more memorable than the *Portrait of a Man* from Cefalù [cat. 3]), what fifteenth-century humanist critics referred to as "the movements of the mind"—the interior life behind the painted mask of so many Renaissance portraits. His achievement may be seen as a first step toward the famous, incipient smile of the *Mona Lisa.*

Antonello appears also as the creator of indelible, deeply emotive images of Christ as the Man of Sorrows. In these extraordinary pictures the viewer is placed in the closest possible proximity to a palpable, physical likeness of suffering, transforming the very terms of private devotional experience. To set off these images he invariably painted a fictive parapet with an illusionistically rendered piece of creased paper attached by sealing wax. Usually the *cartellino,* as it is most often termed, contains his signature—a detail Antonello seems to have taken over from Italian, possibly Paduan, rather than Netherlandish practice and used both to give further emphasis to the concept of painting as mimesis and to assert himself as the author of these moving works. Two of the paintings in the exhibition—a double-sided image of the Madonna and Child with a Franciscan donor and a Christ as the Man of Sorrows (cat. 1) viewed behind Gothic tracery, and one of Saint Jerome in a landscape with, on its recto, another Christ as the Man of Sorrows (cat. 2)—are recent additions to Antonello's oeuvre and may help to solve the riddles of his complex formation.

At the center of this small but exquisite group of pictures we are uniquely fortunate to have one of the most compelling and mysterious of all paintings produced in the fifteenth century: a work that, taken by itself, would do honor to any artist—the *Virgin Annunciate* from the Galleria Regionale della Sicilia in Palermo (cat. 6). It has, without apology or exaggeration, been compared to Leonardo da Vinci's *Mona Lisa* (Musée du Louvre, Paris), and as with that painting there is really nothing like it. Make no mistake, the quality of imagination at work is an exalted one. Once seen, this relatively small picture—it measures only 45 by 34.5 centimeters—haunts the imagination, not as a static image but as a living presence. The young Virgin—she is no more than thirteen or fourteen years old—is at once distant but real, tender but aloof, her plain but not unbeautiful features those of a simple, dark-eyed Mediterranean girl. This maiden does not address us directly. Rather, she is shown behind a lectern set on a table with an open prayer book, the pages of which refuse to lie flat. She is modestly veiled in a woolen blue fabric that falls in large, heavy folds. With her left hand she modestly pinches the edges of the veil across her chest. Her eyes are demurely lowered, gazing at an unseen presence below and to her right, as she extends one hand in a complexly foreshortened gesture of acceptance. The corner of the diagonally placed desk seems to break through the picture plane, making the dark, silent, sacred space that this sublimely self-possessed young woman inhabits impinge on the world of the viewer that her presence sanctifies. We would be right to assume that her gesture is in response to the words of an unseen angel bearing the news that she shall bear a son who will be the Savior of the world, but it seems to me in the highest degree unlikely that Antonello intended this magical image as part of a conventional diptych or that he ever painted a companion panel with an angel bearing the divine message. Rather, he has situated the viewer in the archangel Gabriel's position and, in so doing, elicits from each of us a cued response. To understand that response, we must imagine the picture hanging not in a museum gallery but in the bedroom of a patrician palace in Palermo, and its viewer not as a member of our predominantly secular society, for whom the appreciation of religious art may require an act of conscious suppression of prejudices and the willingness to confront a world of feelings and assumptions different from our own, but as a longtime devotee of the Virgin who each morning and night kneels momentarily to offer a prayer—perhaps of thanksgiving for blessings received or a supplication for something hoped for. By making this act of the imagination we will begin to apprehend that this is a vital, communicative image before which prayers and supplications were made, and that Antonello has created a picture that uniquely responds to this world of private devotional experience. Some viewers may even possibly recall that the most famous of all Catholic religious devotions was the rosary, which in the fifteenth century had still not taken on its final form. The first words of the repeated versical in the rosary are those of the heavenly salutation: Ave Maria Gratia Plena—Hail Mary Full of Grace—and these are the words that must have been repeatedly directed to this holy maiden, whose almost plebeian features can now be seen as central to its function. In uttering these words, the viewer-worshiper imaginatively assumes the place of the unseen angel, and he or she is no less assured of the Virgin's response. This is, then, an image that was made to sanctify private prayer, but it is also a transforming tour de force of artistic imagination.

For the privilege of standing before this exalted painting we owe a deep debt of gratitude to the Foundation for Italian Art and Culture for approaching the Cultural Commissioner of the Sicilian Region and undertaking complex negotiations, as well as to the ministry for generously facilitating the loan of this panel and the two from Messina and Cefalù, none of which has ever been seen in America. I am also grateful to the Wildenstein gallery for arranging for the inclusion of the little-known, double-sided early work by Antonello.

THE LIFE AND WORK OF ANTONELLO DA MESSINA

Gioacchino Barbera

With the following illuminating and evocative words, Roberto Longhi (1953) perfectly defined both Antonello's geniality and his greatness, particularly in the cultural environment of fifteenth-century Sicily: "Antonello. A name that asserts itself with the urgency of great individuality, especially given the time when he worked; that urgency serves, however, not to separate him from this context but rather to increase our sense of his achievement as never before. His prominence in Sicilian society is especially remarkable when one realizes that his first successes in Messina came at the same time as Tommaso de Vigilia was working in Palermo, in fact, but perhaps even before that, as the Sicilian donkey carts were carrying the last Flamboyant Gothic retables up to their hilltop churches. Antonello's place in Sicily was like Masaccio's in Florence, but Masaccio had an initial advantage in that he could study a more modern, and simpler history near by." The essay that follows, taken in part from my own recent work, is an attempt to synthesize and explain, broadly, the very complicated philological problems—many of which are still the subject of scholarly debate—as well as the now well-established evidence we have about events in the career of this artist, who was one of the great protagonists of Italian and European art of the Renaissance.

Messina in the Fifteenth Century, and Antonello's Family and Workshop

The triumph of the centralized authority of the mercantile class over a more isolated feudalistic society assured that Messina would, from the beginning of the fifteenth century, enjoy a long period of prosperity. This prosperity also reinforced its political stability and encouraged the natural disposition of the seaport toward trade. The city was a flourishing center for the warehousing and distribution of goods such as sugar and spices that were exported from the East to Flanders, and it also made the products of the South Italian mainland available to the whole of the Mediterranean market. Among the more important of these commodities were textiles—linen, silk, and fustian (or twilled cotton). Messina also produced wine, cotton, and sugar and maintained a shipbuilding industry, which was essential to a seaside city. Of all these local activities, however, it was the production of silk that predominated. This industry had developed so quickly that by the beginning of the sixteenth century the Lucchese and Venetian silk manufacturers living in Messina requested that a silk consulate be established in the city, and its mid-August trade fair had gained considerable importance.

Life in Messina unfolded between its two dominant powers, political and religious—the Palazzo Reale, which faced the port, and the Duomo (cathedral), located in the heart of the city. Neighborhoods were organized around the activities, corporations, and delegations of the communities of non-Sicilian and foreign merchants which, along with their shops and workshops, had their own churches, palaces, and traditions. Messina's intense relationships with the Mediterranean world—and, especially, its political ties with Catalonia—enriched the artistic culture of the city, which, since it had no strong, indigenous tradition, developed by borrowing diverse elements from these various influences.

Art in Messina, in the Early Quattrocento, reflected a mixture of the International Gothic style imported from Naples—an example of which is still visible in the cathedral portal sculpted by Baboccio da Piperno—with a Catalan–Sicilian style that enriched the city's magnificent carved standards and refined goldsmiths' work. Beginning in the middle of the fifteenth century, however, both sculpture and the goldsmiths' art underwent a change, becoming more sensitive to the stylistic repertoire of the Tuscan Renaissance. The development of literary studies represented a further cultural advance, boosted by the diffusion in the West of Greek culture after the fall of Constantinople. Equally important was the introduction of printing in Messina in the 1460s by Heinrich Alding, making it a thriving center for the production of books illustrated with woodcuts. The absence, noted above, of a strong, indigenous artistic tradition, and the fact that Messina was politically and culturally peripheral, despite its economic resources, made the city more closely dependent on Naples, which, especially under Alfonso of Aragon at mid-century, was to become the most important center for the figurative arts in the south of Italy, bringing together the diverse influences of Flanders, Burgundy, and Provence.

When Antonello began to work in Messina—most likely in the 1440s—there was little stimulation for a young artist in that fairly heterogeneous and old-fashioned town. The exception was the presence in Messina of Netherlandish or Netherlandish-style paintings, which had arrived in the city through trade with Flanders. Another source of inspiration was Neapolitan painting, which reflected the influence of the Netherlandish works that had been imported by King Alfonso.

Antonello's family and its business activities are documented in archival sources in Messina dating from the early fifteenth century. His grandfather Michele owned a brigantine, and his grandmother Annuzza's will of 1438 left a house to her son Giovanni (Antonello's father), who was a *mazonus*—somewhere between a master mason and a marble cutter. Antonello's mother, Garita (Margherita ?), was still alive when her son died in 1479. The family was well integrated into the business and trade communities in Messina and its members well placed in a city that was an obligatory stop for shipping traffic in the Mediterranean; merchants arrived there from many destinations to take advantage of the opportunities to embark on a new profession.

It is not certain exactly when Antonello was born, but for a variety of reasons it most likely was between 1425 and 1430. By at least 1457, he had established a workshop in Messina. Since there is nothing to contradict the humanist Pietro Summonte's proposal that Antonello trained with Niccolò Colantonio (about 1420–after 1460) in Naples shortly after the coronation of Alfonso of Aragon in 1443, we can only assume that the young artist left Messina for the capital of the new kingdom, under circumstances still unknown to us, at some time around that date. The cultural vitality that emanated from the Neapolitan court, enriching the kingdom's leading artistic centers, was probably a decisive factor in Antonello's decision to depart for Naples. At the same time, the restrictions imposed by the local scene, which we can glean from surviving documents, undoubtedly also contributed to the young painter's decision to leave his native city.

It might also be significant that Antonello's departure for Naples coincides almost exactly with the presence in Palermo of a skilled and cosmopolitan anonymous master, who was probably from Valencia and whose work certainly had an impact on the artistic production of the island. This artist frescoed a large *Triumph of Death* on a wall of the Palazzo Sclafani, which, under the patronage of King Alfonso, had been converted to a hospital. (That fresco has now been elegantly reinstalled by Carlo Scarpa in the Galleria Regionale della Sicilia in the Palazzo Abatellis.)

Antonello's workshop was, in any case, the first and only one to be successful in all of eastern Sicily and

Calabria, and in time included the artist's brother, brother-in-law, and son, as well as occasional apprentices, among its members. Antonello received a number of commissions from the cities of Reggio Calabria, Caltagirone, Catania, Noto (where, documents tell us, he went in person), Randazzo, and Palazzolo Acreide. Antonello's sojourn in Venice, and the pictures he executed there, are tangible evidence of his fame and prestige, which had spread beyond Southern Italy. This was likely a result of international trade as well as of an appreciation for the "Northern" style—that is, the Netherlandish technique—which Antonello had learned from Colantonio and which was greatly admired in most contemporary cultural centers.

Nevertheless, it must be admitted that Antonello appears to have had few major commissions in his native Sicily (even taking into consideration that many works may have been lost in earthquakes or through indifference and neglect). Indeed, it seems that Messina did not have a well-to-do class of inhabitants who would have felt the need to affirm and promote their status by commissioning works of art. According to archival sources, Antonello's Sicilian clients, instead, were mostly confraternities, and these often were in competition with one another. They required devotional standards to carry in their processions, and their commissions involved the repetition of the same images, made from the same immutable models. This may be the reason that Antonello sought work in Venice, where several of his portraits of noblemen and merchants—who had been to Messina—were both known and appreciated. His stay there was brief, but it bore exceptional fruit, not because of the number of works he produced but rather because of their exceptional quality, as compared with his earlier efforts. It is not known whether his Venetian sojourn was curtailed because of ill health—Antonello, in fact, died at a young age, just a few years later—or as a result of the hostility of his competitors, especially Giovanni Bellini.

Although Antonello's early death, followed almost immediately by that of his son Jacobello, at first diminished and then virtually destroyed the output of his workshop—it had been taken over by his nephews and other relatives with little talent—from that point on Messina looked toward more modern artistic and cultural developments. Of the remaining family, only Salvo d'Antonio, Antonello's nephew, was able to keep up with the livelier currents in Southern Italian art. The arrival in Messina in the early sixteenth century first of Cesare da Sesto (1477–1523) and then of Polidoro da Caravaggio (about 1499–1543), both Northern Italian artists, provides tangible evidence of an ongoing artistic vitality that had its roots in Antonello's work.

Antonello's Training and Early Work

It is now widely accepted by scholars that Antonello trained in the Neapolitan workshop of Colantonio, a master steeped in the Netherlandish style that was then dominant in that lively southern capital. Much of the city's artistic vibrancy was due to the presence of artists or works of art from Provençal France and from Spain, who arrived there during the reign of King René of Anjou (1438–42) and then of Alfonso of Aragon (1442–58). Antonello's apprenticeship in Naples in all probability occurred between 1445 and 1455. He returned to Messina sometime in the 1450s—the first surviving archival document in which his name appears is dated March 5, 1457, and records the execution of a standard for the confraternity of San Michele dei Gerbini in Reggio Calabria—where he founded a workshop that produced banners and devotional images for churches and confraternities; these objects, now known only from archival notices, were much in demand by local patrons.

The reconstruction of this early period in Antonello's career is largely hypothetical, and is based on the attribution of two works, the *Virgin Annunciate* (Pinacoteca Civica, Como) and the *Virgin Reading* (Forti degli Adimari Collection, Venice), both of which are closely linked to Colantonio's style, as well as of the *Saint Zosimus* in the cathedral in Siracusa, although there is still considerable doubt about the attribution of this picture. These works are painted in what is essentially the Netherlandish style invented by Jan van Eyck, which was disseminated in Naples by Colantonio and by the paintings of contemporary Provençal and Spanish artists then well known in the city.

The Provençal influence is important in any understanding of the cultural diversity and artistic exchange that characterized Aragonese Naples in the 1460s. King René's almost constant presence in Provence after his departure from Naples in 1442, and the establishment of strong economic ties, encouraged a give-and-take relationship—including the exchange of artists—between Southern France and the great coastal cities of the Aragonese kingdom. From one side of the Mediterranean to the other there was a flurry of cultural interaction, as demonstrated, for example, by the peregrinations of the sculptor Francesco Laurana (d. before 1502), who went from Naples, where he worked on Alfonso's monumental Triumphal Arch (the entrance to the Castelnuovo), to Provence, at the behest of King René, and then to Sicily and again to Naples before finally returning again to Provence.

One might credit Laurana's presence in Sicily to the growing interest of the island's leading feudal families in a Renaissance style that had been introduced into Southern Italy with the first phase of work on Alfonso's Triumphal Arch. In painting, a similar interest developed in Northern European art, manifested in the work of the Provençal and Spanish artists. Always with the caveat that paintings are susceptible to being moved or lost—and, thus, that our evidence may very well be incomplete—it seems clear that, Antonello's output aside, the best Sicilian works from this period that survive on the island exhibit strong connections with both Spain and Provence. These include *The Coronation of the Virgin* by an artist influenced by Jaume Huguet (about 1415–before 1492) and by Enguerrand Quarton (about 1420–1466), formerly at Corleone (now in the Palazzo Abatellis), as well as paintings in several interior regions that were flourishing artistically at the time, such as Militello in the Val di Catania—a fief of the powerful Barresi family—among them a *Saint Peter Enthroned* and a double-sided *Crucifixion* in Piazza Armerina. The great anonymous artist who painted these pictures, now known as the Master of the Piazza Armerina Cross, worked in a Provençal style. He likely executed his works in Piazza Armerina, or sent them on, a few years before Antonello's (now lost) altarpiece arrived in the nearby wealthy town of Caltagirone, which also had a *Trinity* derived from a work by Rogier van der Weyden. Antonello may have received the commission for this altarpiece upon his return to Messina from Noto, and he was paid the enormous sum of forty-five gold *once* for it.

Antonello must have made another trip to the mainland at the end of the 1450s. In January 1460 he returned to Messina by ship from Amantea in Calabria, accompanied by many family members and personal effects, suggesting that he had been on a long voyage that perhaps also took him far away.

Although the source of his inspiration is not clear, Antonello's style in the 1460s certainly reflects the influence of the culture of mainland Italy and especially of the Tuscan painters Fra Angelico (about 1395–1455) and Piero della Francesca (about 1406/12–1492); however, it also exhibits some affinity with the works of French and Provençal artists such as Jean Fouquet and the aforementioned Quarton, who, in turn, were stylistically closely linked with these Italian Renaissance masters. At that time, Rome was the nearest city in which an artist from the south might see contemporary works by Fra Angelico, Piero, and Fouquet, and the most likely hypothesis is that Antonello may, indeed, have traveled to Rome.

While all of Antonello's documented works from this period are now lost, his surviving paintings demonstrate the continual enrichment of his artistic vision, his rigorous use of perspective, and his interest in the synthesis of formal elements, especially the relationship between figures and space. This body of work includes the *Saint Nicholas* for the church of San Nicola dei Gentiluomini in Messina (now lost, but known from an old copy, perhaps by Antonino Giuffrè, a follower of Antonello, in the cathedral in Milazzo, and from sketches made by the great art historian and connoisseur Giovan Battista Cavalcaselle during his trip to Sicily in the second half of the nineteenth century); the *Salting Madonna* (National Gallery, London); the refined, slightly later *Virgin Reading* (The Walters Art Museum, Baltimore); the *Crucifixion* from Sibiu (now in the Muzeul Național de Artă, Bucharest); and the two small panels of *Saint Jerome in the Desert* and *Three Angels Visiting Abraham* (Museo della Magna Grecia, Reggio Calabria). From these works it is clear that without abandoning his interest in the luminous realism of Netherlandish art, Antonello's visual style had become Italianized.

It is precisely in these years that Antonello reached the peak of his achievement in his synthesis of an analytical, Northern approach with an Italian treatment of perspective, blending chronicle and history in painted form. Already in the *Salting Madonna,* and despite its strong Netherlandish style, he succeeded in transforming an image of a typical Sicilian woman through a process of formal abstraction learned from Piero della Francesca and from Quarton. The sitter in his *Portrait of a Man* (cat. 3)—the so-called "Unknown Sailor," perhaps the earliest of Antonello's surviving portraits—is given carefully individualized Sicilian features and a face "in whose smile, somewhere between astonished and threatening, is condensed the essential ambiguity of that fascinating and terrible island" (Zeri 1976).

The *Crucifixion* from Sibiu raises the same issues. While the draperies of the mourning figures at the foot of the cross are painted in a lingering Northern style and the foreground seems to fall away in a recognizably Netherlandish manner, the delicate but firm nude figures of Christ and the thieves evoke Tuscan painting, and the work of Fra Angelico in particular. They are lucidly arranged in the pictorial space, the planes of which are clearly articulated in relation to the background view of Messina and the Straits, where the mountains seem to blend into the sea.

Antonello's Hypothetical Voyage in the Late 1460s and His Work in Sicily (1470–74)

The surviving documents in Sicily make no mention of Antonello after 1465, except for a 1471 notice of his presence in Noto to execute a standard (now lost) for the confraternity of the Holy Spirit. From then until 1475, when he was certainly in Venice, Antonello worked primarily in Sicily. The lack of archival sources from the second half of the 1460s is hardly evidence (especially given the number of documents lost in the various vicissitudes Messina has undergone) that he was absent from the island. The fact, however, that Antonello's work from about 1470 on is iconographically, thematically, as well as stylistically innovative suggests that he had altered his painting style in a profound way.

Based on these circumstances and on a careful examination of his surviving work from this period, scholars have suggested that Antonello returned to the mainland, this time visiting Central and Northern Italy. Such a journey would have allowed him to make a more precise study of Piero della Francesca's work in Perugia and Urbino, and it might also have led to Antonello's first contact in Padua and Venice with the paintings of Andrea Mantegna and Giovanni Bellini while reviving his interest in Netherlandish painting.

The only work by Antonello to have remained continuously in Messina is the Saint Gregory polyptych, signed and dated 1473 (damaged in the 1908 earthquake, it is missing its original wood frame, which undoubtedly was carved in a Late Gothic style, as well as the central panel of its upper register; based on the mediocre surviving copies of the polyptych, it is reasonable to suppose that this panel represented either a *Pietà* or an image of the dead Christ supported by angels).

Antonello's altarpiece clearly reflects the influence of Piero's Saint Anthony polyptych in Perugia, and the arrangement of the upper panels of the *Annunciation* derives from Giovanni Bellini's Saint Vincent Ferrer polyptych painted in the second half of the 1460s for the church of Santi Giovanni e Paolo in Venice. Of Paduan derivation is the small scroll—or *cartellino*—on the central panel, with the artist's signature and the date, which also appears in the portraits and in the various *Ecce Homo* panels of the same years, while the more convincing rendering of space and the artist's increasing interest in a perspective scheme that relies on pure geometric units reflect the influence of Piero's work in general. The polyptych as a whole is unified by a limpid light that melds its Netherlandish elements—apparent in the faces, in the angels who hold the crown, and in the arabesque-patterned fabric—and the old-fashioned gold ground of the panels required by the patron Sister Fabria Cirino, Abbess of the convent of Santa Maria extra Moenia, whose family's coat of arms is visible near Saint Gregory's feet.

The three pinnacles representing the Doctors of the Church (*Saint Gregory, Saint Jerome,* and *Saint Augustine*)—now in the Galleria Regionale della Sicilia, Palazzo Abatellis, Palermo—are perhaps part of a "carved altarpiece" ("icona intagliata") made for the church of San Giacomo in Caltagirone and documented in 1473. It is possible that this altarpiece also included a *Saint Benedict* (now in the Castello Sforzesco, Milan) and the two panels of the *Madonna and Child with Angels* and *Saint John the Baptist,* both now in the Galleria degli Uffizi, Florence, and among the most recent additions to the artist's oeuvre. Alternatively, these panels may have been undertaken somewhat earlier than the Saint Gregory polyptych discussed above, although both works reveal the marked influence of an Italian Renaissance culture on Antonello's style. Other works painted at the same time, however, reflect the artist's renewed interest in Netherlandish art and include the *Annunciation* executed in 1474 for the Church of the Annunciation in Palazzolo Acreide (now in the Galleria Regionale di Palazzo Bellomo, Siracusa); the *Saint Jerome in His Study* (fig. 1; difficult to date, although it has been assigned in the recent literature to the artist's mature period) and the *Salvator Mundi* (both now in the National Gallery, London); as well as several portraits.

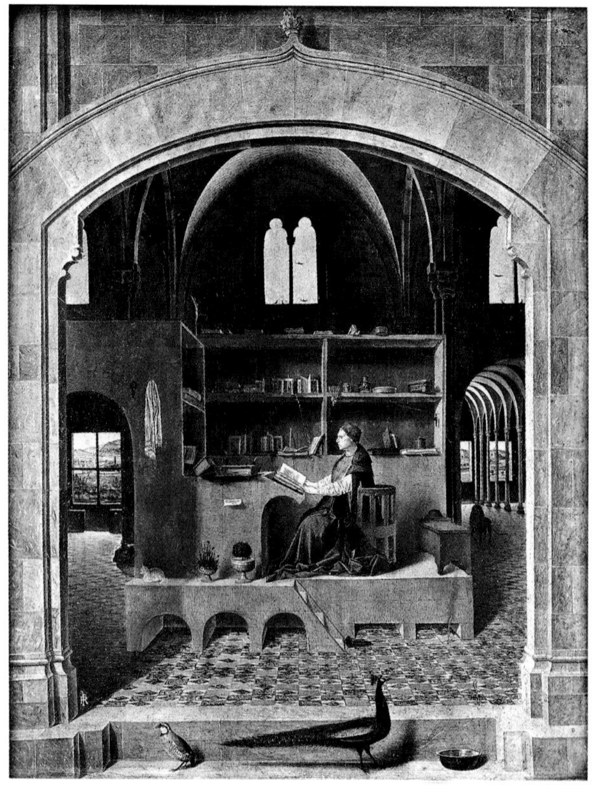

Figure 1. Antonello da Messina. *Saint Jerome in His Study*. About 1475. Oil on panel. National Gallery, London (NG1418)

It is not known what precipitated this revival of Netherlandish motifs in Antonello's work; the trip to Flanders mentioned by Vasari and often believed to have occurred in these years may be a plausible explanation, but one that remains in the realm of speculation. There is no question, however, that the paintings mentioned above display a remarkable affinity with the works of the Netherlandish painter Petrus Christus, a pupil of Jan van Eyck, who, in turn, was strongly affected by Italian art. Antonello's iconographically innovative series on the *Ecce Homo*—an early example of which can be dated to about 1470 (cat. 4)—and the portraits he executed in this period all display the influence of Netherlandish painting. The artist's new approach to landscape was also inspired by the art of Flanders. Pale blue skies, expanses of water, and lush green hills and valleys make up the backgrounds in such works as the Siracusa *Annunciation,* while the interior setting of the London *Saint Jerome* represents a purely Netherlandish sensibility. The artist's technique is ever more limpid and precise, his use of transparent oil glazes over tempera approximating the refinement and preciosity of Netherlandish painting.

The framing of the scene in the London *Saint Jerome* employs Catalan Gothic motifs, and the painting's intense focus on detail (as, for example, the symbolic animals in the foreground, the small plants in majolica pots, the books and other objects on the shelves) seems to point to a Northern taste, yet, even here, the rendering of the small figure of the seated saint, carefully delineated in profile and as intent on his studies as a humanist scholar, is decidedly Italian in character and stylistically very different from the work of a Netherlandish master. This undated picture—variously attributed in the past to Hans Memling, Albrecht Dürer, Jan van Eyck, and Jacometto Veneziano—is identifiable with a work seen by Marcantonio Michiel in the house of the Venetian collector Antonio Pasqualino in 1529 (Michiel wrote: "the small panel of St. Jerome who, dressed in his cardinal's robes, reads in his study, is believed by some to come from the hand of Antonello from Messina, although more actually give it to Gianes [Jan van Eyck] or to Memling, the old Northern painter: and so it shows that style, even though the face is finished in an Italian manner as if it had been painted by the hand of Jacometto").

Similar issues surround the *Salvator Mundi* (or *Christ Blessing*) in London (National Gallery). The problems in dating this work have been much discussed and stem from an internal contradiction in the date indicated in the inscription on the painted *cartellino,* which can be read as 1460 or 1475, as well as from the *pentimenti* visible even to the naked eye. Yet, Christ's extraordinary gesture of blessing, in which the right hand is held low and turned toward the viewer, reveals a sophisticated knowledge of perspective characteristic of Antonello's work in the 1470s and that culminated in the paintings he executed in Venice in 1475–76.

However, even the most consistently Netherlandish paintings, such as the Siracusa *Annunciation,* convey a sense of space and scale that is typically Italian. (It is worth noting that the charm of this work, its original beauty, is still intact, despite the large losses it has suffered: these already were evident when the picture was rediscovered in 1907, but no restorations—even the most recent, in 1987—have been able to repair them.) The same is true of Antonello's portraits, which, although close to the manner of Petrus Christus, are indisputably "Renaissance" in style in their synthetic plasticity and sharp psychological presence. The series of *Ecce Homo* panels (cat. 4; Galleria Alberoni, Piacenza; Galleria Nazionale di Palazzo Spinola, Genoa; and formerly, Kunsthistorisches Museum, Vienna), all of which can be dated to the 1470s, reveal the influence of Piero della Francesca and of Mantegna, but they also display a more solid handling of Christ's body, convincingly anchored in space and, at the same time, imbued with a restrained pathos.

Antonello as a Portrait Painter

It is not known when Antonello began to paint portraits, but it seems unlikely that this occurred before the late 1460s. It should be emphasized that he immediately adopted a Netherlandish portrait model: a bust-length figure seen frontally or in slightly three-quarter view, dressed in ordinary clothing and placed against a dark ground. While Antonello remained largely unaffected by the humanistic portrait type inspired by ancient medals, coins, and cameos, on which courtly and idealized sitters were represented in strict profile, such works had a decisive influence on the development of portrait painting in Italy and elsewhere in Europe.

The portrait as an autonomous genre, rare in fourteenth-century painting, developed over the course of the Quattrocento, and, until the late fifteenth century, it was the profile portrait in particular that predominated in Italy. Examples of the type are the portraits of the donors of altarpieces that were incorporated in the scenes at the feet of the Virgin or the saints; depicted in profile, from the fourteenth century on, these representations might have served as a precedent for the eventual ubiquity of profile portraits in general. More important in the development of the genre was the humanist climate that prevailed throughout the Italian peninsula in the late fourteenth and early fifteenth centuries, and the revival of interest in ancient coins and medals, with their profile images of emperors. Pisanello, renowned for the quality of the profile portraits on the medals he made, also executed panel paintings in which he represented his subject in profile, and Domenico Veneziano, Piero della Francesca, and Antonio del Pollaiuolo all depicted their sitters in profile as well.

Bust-length frontal or three-quarter-view portraits are also found in Italian art: not only are portrait sculptures usually meant to be seen frontally but, often, portraits of specific individuals are included in fresco scenes otherwise crowded with figures in a variety of poses. A well-known example of this type is Masaccio's so-called *Sagra del Carmine,* with its procession of figures; this fresco perhaps was the direct source for the unique work (Musée du Louvre, Paris) attributed to Paolo Uccello, which contains multiple bust-length portraits of Giotto, Uccello, Donatello, Manetti, and Brunelleschi, all but the last represented frontally or in three-quarter profile. A bust-length portrait by the Florentine Andrea del Castagno also shows the sitter facing front (National Gallery of Art, Washington, D.C.).

The Northern Italian painter Andrea Mantegna, too, abandoned the humanist formula of the medallion profile portrait in his frontal image of Cardinal Ludovico Trevisan (Staatliche Museen, Berlin) of 1459–60, but Mantegna's portrait of Cardinal Francesco Gonzaga (Museo e Gallerie Nazionale di Capodimonte, Naples) shows the subject in profile; in his portrait of Cardinal Carlo de' Medici (Galleria degli Uffizi, Florence), Mantegna returned to a frontal view. All of these works possess a monumentality of effect, their idealized subjects presented in a heroic and historical context.

In Northern Europe, Jan van Eyck had introduced a portrait type that became popular in Flanders, especially in the part that belonged to the Duchy of Burgundy, from at least the 1420s on. As a portraitist he was especially interested in rendering the sitter's physiognomy, the details of his or her clothing, and the individual characteristics of the person being portrayed, and Netherlandish portraits of this type were soon disseminated throughout France and Spain. In the early 1430s, van Eyck executed several bust-length, frontal portraits (the so-called *Tymotheus,* or *Portrait of a Young Man,* and *The Man with a Red Turban,* both now in the National Gallery, London; and the *Portrait of Cardinal Albergati,* now in the Kunsthistorisches Museum, Vienna), as well as the celebrated full-length double portrait known as "*The Arnolfini Portrait*" (National Gallery, London), which depicts a wealthy Tuscan merchant and his consort in a domestic setting—their bedchamber—amid an almost overwhelming profusion of everyday detail.

The popularity of this descriptive, technically precise type of portrait spread from Northern Europe to France and Spain, and found a ready audience among the powerful merchant classes, whose members enjoyed seeing their features carefully rendered along with the clothing and furniture that conveyed their social status. The Arnolfini were Italian tradesmen, and, like other businessmen and merchants from Florence, Genoa, or Venice, would easily have been able to import such portraits "in a Northern style." The political, commercial, and artistic ties that linked Southern Italy and Sicily with Flanders and, especially, with Spain and France, make it likely that Netherlandish-style portraits prevailed there as early as the middle of the fifteenth century.

The portraits by Petrus Christus, one of van Eyck's students, dating from the 1440s, seem most closely to anticipate Antonello's style. However, the affinities shared by these two artists do not stop with their portrait paintings, although the stylistic similarities are perhaps the most explicit in that genre. This suggests the possibility that Antonello may have been inspired to adopt a Northern style of portraiture after seeing a work by Petrus Christus. In any case, Antonello adopted this style of portrait painting at a fortuitous moment in the late 1460s, when the city of Messina was dominated by a baronial class that applied the income from its land holdings to commercial ends, and thus was open to indulging in painted portraits.

The same held true in Venice, where much of what survives of Antonello's portrait production does so because it was executed there or at least was destined for the inhabitants of that city. There are a few works that are certainly Sicilian (these include the *Portrait of a Man* [cat. 3], probably the first in the series, and a *Portrait of a Young Man* [now in Berlin], whose date is usually read as 1478). Archival documents in Venice and other Northern Italian centers also testify to the Sicilian painter's success as a portraitist.

From the Netherlandish examples that inspired his work Antonello borrowed the format of the half-length figure in three-quarter profile, the depiction of contemporary dress, and the intensely focused illumination. However, over time, he began to simplify these Netherlandish models, toning down their insistent realism and microscopic attention to detail and replacing these qualities with a more synthetic and abstract monumentality, in keeping with the tradition of Italian portraiture. With the exception of the portrait in Berlin (where the landscape and the sky may have been added early on, inspired by the popularity of Memling's portraits), their simplified backgrounds have a compact, dark atmosphere unlike the settings of the majority of Petrus Christus's portraits as well as of those by later Netherlandish painters. Synthesizing the realism of Northern portraiture with the measured idealism of Italian examples in the early 1470s, Antonello invented a new portrait type that was the most modern in style of any on the Italian peninsula. For several years he was the indisputable master of the genre, and he had a profound influence on the leading exponents of Venetian portraiture, from Giovanni Bellini to Alvise Vivarini and from Bartolomeo Montagna to Jacometto Veneziano.

The Ecce Homo *Theme*

Representations of the *Ecce Homo*—the isolated, half-length figure of Christ—occur most often in Netherlandish art in double representations of the Triumphant Christ (*Christus triumphans*) and the Suffering Christ (*Christus patiens*). Examples of Christ triumphant were not entirely absent from Italian art, but their incidence was unusual, and only isolated works with this theme exist before the second half of the fifteenth century. In Italian Gothic painting the blessing or triumphant Christ generally occupies a pinnacle atop a polyptych or, very rarely, the keys of the vault over the crossing in the nave of a church, assuming a dominant position at the apex of a fresco cycle. In instances of the latter, Christ, in a reprise of Byzantine iconography, assumes the form of the Supreme Judge, blessing with his right hand while holding a book in his left hand. However, there seem to be no images of the *Christus patiens* in Italian painting of the fourteenth and early fifteenth centuries, although depictions of the dead Christ, usually represented as a half-length figure propped up in his sarcophagus with his arms crossed over his abdomen, do exist, and typically occupy the center panel of the predella of a polyptych. It is very unusual to find representations of Christ other than on a predella, even if such images were intended as part of a much larger complex. The opposite was true in Northern countries, where isolated paintings of the *Christus triumphans* and the *Christus patiens* appeared by the first half of the fifteenth century; the theme was widely disseminated, giving rise, in the 1460s, to the development of the *Ecce Homo* type.

Antonello left us a sole yet extraordinary image of the Triumphant Christ: the *Christ Blessing* (now in London). However, he took up the theme of the *Ecce Homo* in painting several times, and in two different iconographic variations: the first, a conventional interpretation, showed Christ crowned with thorns, being presented to the populace by Pontius Pilate; the second depicted Christ at the Column. Regardless of whether the Sicilian painter adapted this subject from Netherlandish painting, he ended up by translating it into a wholly Italian idiom, his figure types inspired by Piero della Francesca's statuesque nudes—examples include the *Saint Sebastian* in the Polyptych of the Misericordia (Museo Civico, Sansepolcro) or the Christ of the *Flagellation* (Galleria Nazionale delle Marche, Urbino)—and by the works by those Northern Italian masters influenced by Mantegna. If one excludes two double-sided, small panels—the first identified by Federico Zeri as an *Ecce Homo* with a *Saint Jerome in the Desert* on the reverse (cat. 2) and the other as a *Madonna and Child, with a Praying Franciscan Donor,* and, on the verso, an *Ecce Homo* (cat. 1), with the latter dated tentatively to the second half of the 1460s because of the Catalan-style frame around the niche—it is significant that Antonello's first independent version of the *Ecce Homo* (cat. 4) is not earlier than 1470, the date once thought to have been legible on the *cartellino.* All the other examples are either firmly dated to after 1470 or appear to be of that date because of incontrovertible stylistic evidence.

As mentioned above, Antonello likely made a first trip to Northern Italy at the end of the 1460s, and during this voyage he must have come to know Piero della Francesca's work in Perugia and Urbino, as well as that of the school of Squarcione in Padua—especially the paintings by Mantegna in that city. In the much-damaged New York *Ecce Homo* (cat. 4), there is a painted *cartellino* on the parapet that clearly derives from this Paduan tradition, and yet the panel is also stylistically the closest of the series to Netherlandish examples. The pose of the figure is fully frontal, the slight torsion in the torso indicated by a subtle movement of the shoulders and by the inclined head.

The degree of movement of the figure in the Genoa *Ecce Homo* (Galleria Nazionale di Palazzo Spinola) is more accentuated, and thus the composition is spatially more complex. The date on the *cartellino* (painted, rather unusually, on the original frame) is now illegible, but the more formal disposition of the nude figure suggests that the work is later, even if only slightly, than the panel in New York. One should also note the novel iconographic detail of the bound hands of Christ—a motif that will recur in subsequent works.

The date on the painted *cartellino* of the parapet in the *Ecce Homo* in Piacenza (Galleria Alberoni) is also hard to decipher, although it is usually read as 1473. The torsion of this figure is even more marked, while the profusion of elaborate details, from the crown of thorns and the rough cord that casts delicate shadows on Christ's perfect nude form to the exceptional rendering of the hair, tears, and drops of blood, demonstrates Antonello's absolute mastery of his subject. Here, too, the iconography has been enriched with a new element: this is no longer an image of Christ brought before the people but, instead, a specific depiction of Christ bound to the column.

What is now considered to be the latest of Antonello's *Ecce Homo* pictures is known today only through a photograph; the painting disappeared from the storerooms of the Kunsthistorisches Museum in Vienna during World War II, where it had been hidden by the Polish Ostrowskj family. This work also represented Christ at the Column, and the date of 1474—easily read on the *cartellino,* even in the photograph—accords perfectly with the solidly executed nude figure, perhaps a study for the slightly later *Saint Sebastian* (Gemäldegalerie, Dresden).

There are a number of copies and derivations of Antonello's *Ecce Homo* paintings; among the most notable is the panel formerly in the Museo Civico, Novara (it was stolen some decades ago). The representation of the cord falling over the parapet provides a subtle indication of space, and the drops of blood scattered over the figure make this composition the most intensely tragic of the series. The pathos of this picture is, moreover, characteristic of Antonello's late period (it is apparent even in the copies and derivations) and in paintings from his sojourn in Venice, such as the Paris *Christ at the Column* (Musée du Louvre), so close in its devotional tenor to the *Ecce Homo* pictures, and the Madrid *Pietà* (Museo Nacional del Prado), one of the painter's last works.

Antonello in Venice

During his first (undocumented) visit to Venice, Antonello must have acquired some faithful patrons. Moreover, there were certainly Venetian merchants working in Messina as well as men of Sicilian origin in Venice, and it seems likely that one such individual invited the painter, late in 1474, to visit the city on the lagoon, perhaps having been captivated by the rare, formal perfection of his portraits, or by some small panel painting in the Netherlandish style.

The exceedingly high quality of the work Antonello executed in Venice in 1475 and 1476 (he is documented back in Messina in the fall of 1476) suggests, not unreasonably, that his voyage to Venice included new cultural experiences prompted by the additional stops he made along the way; this would explain the evolution in his painting toward an Italian treatment of perspective and a newfound harmony of space, light, and color. He may have stopped in Urbino, to look again at Piero's work (the *Flagellation* and the just completed *Sacra Conversazione* [now in Milan]); in Pesaro, where Giovanni Bellini's large panel of *The Coronation of the Virgin* was newly installed; in Rimini, where a *Pietà* also by Bellini had recently arrived; in Ferrara, to study the works of Piero della Francesca but also of Cosmè Tura and Francesco del Cossa; and in Padua, where the impression left by Mantegna's frescoes and the intarsias by the Lendinara family would have been strong. Antonello must have found himself reexamining the significant trends in Northern Italian painting, which led him to introduce a greater plasticity, a more calculated use of perspective, and an even more glorious

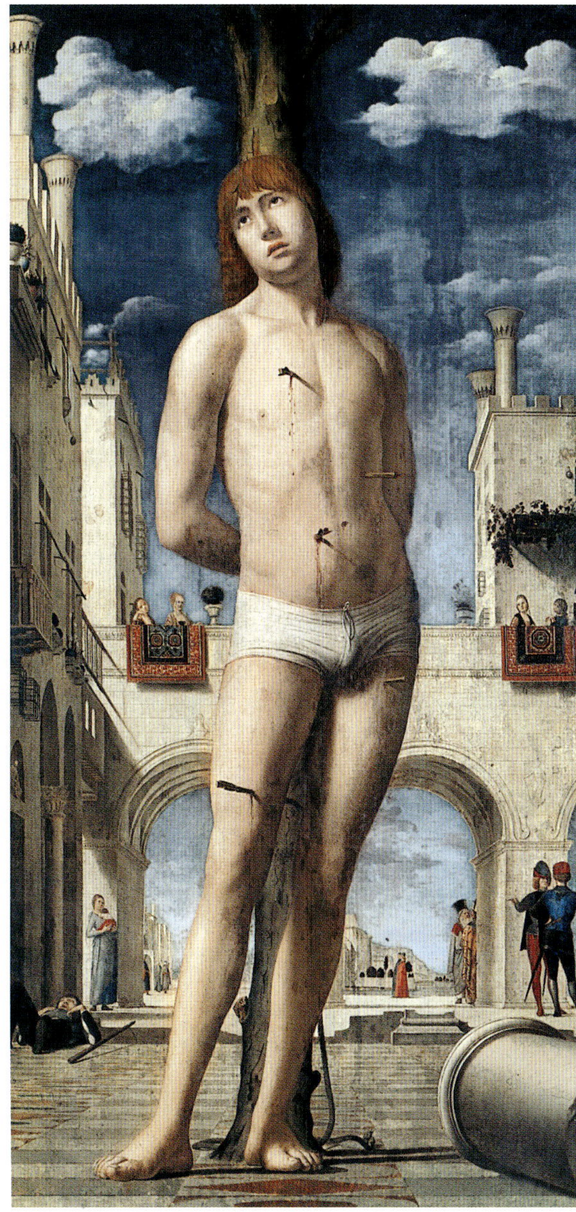

Figure 2. Antonello da Messina. *Saint Sebastian*. 1475–76. Oil, transferred from panel to canvas. Gemäldegalerie, Staatliche Kunstsammlungen, Dresden (inv. 52)

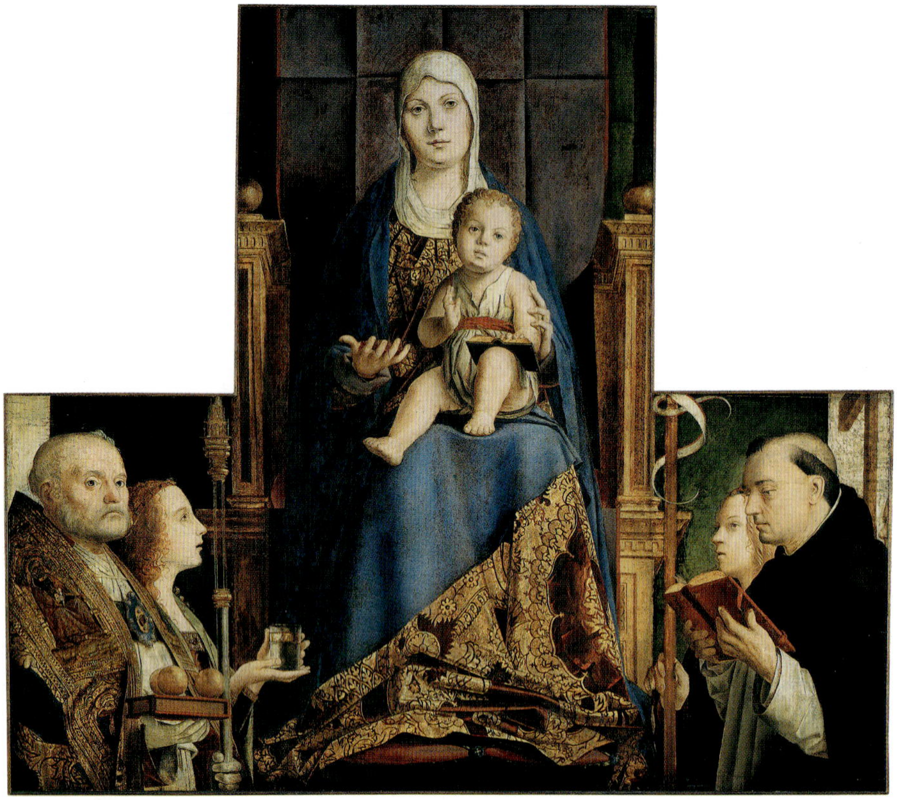

Figure 3. Antonello da Messina. *Madonna and Child, with Saints Nicholas of Bari, Anastasia (?), Ursula, Dominic, and Helena* (from the San Cassiano altarpiece). 1475–76. Oil on panel. Kunsthistorisches Museum, Vienna (Inv. 2574)

luminosity into his work, inspired in large part by contemporary paintings by Bellini. This is most evident in the *Saint Sebastian* (fig. 2), the only surviving panel of a triptych executed for the church of San Giuliano, and in the San Cassiano altarpiece, of which only three fragments from the central section remain (fig. 3). In the latter work, the painter also reprised the iconography of the *sacra conversazione* in the Veneto.

The *Saint Sebastian* is geometrically perfect, but it is also profoundly rooted in reality. The picture combines new developments in perspective with an idealized formal abstraction characteristic of painting in Urbino, Mantua, and Padua. At the same time, Antonello demonstrates the unique ability to render the details of everyday life with a tender radiance that portends the rarefied and enchanted world captured by Carpaccio.

The San Cassiano altarpiece was executed in the eight-month period between August 1475 and April 1476. The splendid quality of the surviving fragments reveal how Antonello sought a gentler rendering of humanity: the features of the figures are softened and are painted with an unusually warm palette, without sacrificing their overall monumentality. However, it is the surprising novelty of the composition that makes this work truly exceptional. The solemn architectural structure is truly Renaissance in spirit—a fully unified space covered by a vault or dome, according to Johannes Wilde's convincing reconstruction (1929). In this space, filled with light and shadow, Antonello placed his saints and the enthroned Madonna and Child.

This painting would remain an important prototype for later artists for three decades; it was imitated by Giovanni Bellini, Bartolomeo Montagna, Cima da Conegliano, Alvise Vivarini, and even Giorgione. Dürer, furthermore, borrowed the florid beauty of Antonello's Madonna in his images of the Virgin. The portraits

Antonello executed in or sent to Venice also played a similar decisive role in the development of the great tradition of Venetian portraiture.

The *Saint Sebastian* and the San Cassiano altarpiece are without doubt among the most stunning accomplishments of Italian painting in the second half of the fifteenth century, but Antonello painted other masterpieces during his brief but intensely active sojourn in Venice, including the (now badly damaged) *Pietà with Three Angels* (Museo Correr, Venice). Clearly inspired by Bellini, this *Pietà* nonetheless reflects the ongoing influence of Netherlandish painting, as in the slender, nude body of Christ; the pointed wings of the angels; and the panoramic landscape, which also includes a nostalgic reference to Antonello's native city in the depiction of the apse of the church of San Francesco. Among his other masterpieces from this period are several portraits (the so-called *Condottiere* [Musée du Louvre, Paris], the *Portrait of a Man in Black* [Museo Thyssen-Bornemisza, Madrid], two additional male portraits [National Gallery, London; and Galleria Borghese, Rome], and two versions of a *Crucifixion* [National Gallery, London; and fig. 4]). The *Crucifixion* in Antwerp is especially admired for the beauty of its landscape and for the torsion of the thieves' bodies, which are rendered in strong foreshortening; while the picture still betrays the perfect illumination and refined detail of Netherlandish painting, it is eminently Italian in its spatial clarity. The precious and enigmatic *Madonna and Child,* commonly known as the *Benson Madonna* (National Gallery of Art, Washington, D.C.)—a work certainly influenced by Bellini—may also be from this period.

Writing in Venice in 1475, Matteo Colazio praised Antonello, on the basis of these Venetian works, as one of the very few artists who, by virtue of his handling of perspective, could compete with the ancients, thus placing him at the head of a group that included Mantegna, the Bellini, Pietro Lombardo, Antonio Riccio, and Bartolomeo Bellano—this is, the elite of the Renaissance masters in the Veneto. Pietro Bon, the patron of the San Cassiano altarpiece, described the as-yet-unfinished work to Duke Galeazzo Maria Sforza as "one of the most excellent painted works either in or outside of Italy."

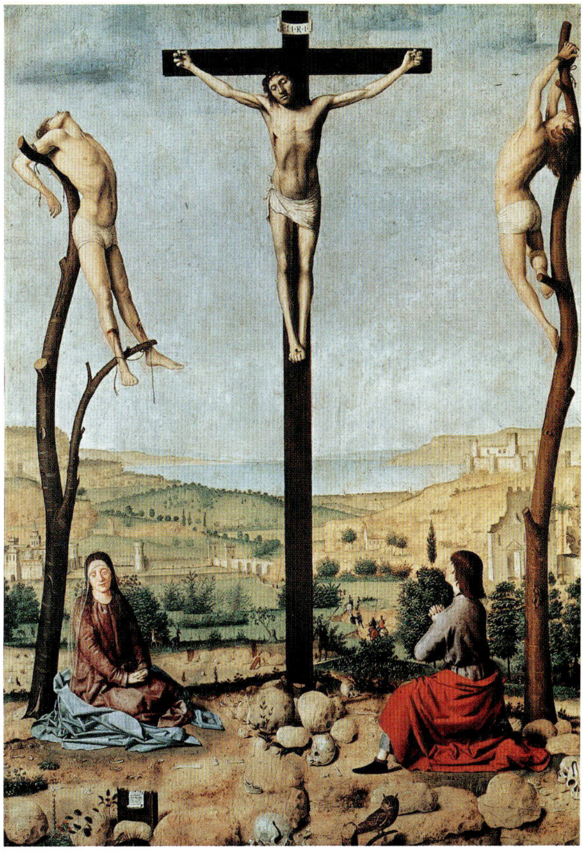

Figure 4. Antonello da Messina. *The Crucifixion*. Oil on panel. Koninklijk Museum voor Schone Kunsten, Antwerp (inv. 4)

Antonello's Return to Messina, His Last Works, and His Following in Sicily

Antonello returned to Messina in the autumn of 1476 after having declined the same duke's invitation to relocate to Milan to take up the position of court portraitist recently left vacant by the death of Zanetto Bugatto. He is documented in Messina in a note, dated September 14, 1476, added at the bottom of a notarial act concerning the last installment paid on the dowry of his daughter Caterinella. From that date until his death in 1479, Antonello headed a very active workshop that employed various members of his family, the most important among them his son Jacobello, who had almost certainly accompanied his father to Venice. His commissions included numerous (now lost) works for Messina and for other towns in Sicily (Ficarra, Catania, Randazzo) that are mentioned in the many surviving documents.

The works from this late period include the superb *Portrait of a Man* (Museo Civico d'Arte Antica, Turin), painted in 1476—his physiognomy so intensely Sicilian—and another portrait, dated 1478 (Gemäldegalerie, Berlin), the well-known *Virgin Annunciate* (cat. 6); and also the moving *Pietà* in the Prado, which, unanimously, is considered to be Antonello's last work, perhaps completed by Jacobello.

There is little to add to what has already been said about the *Virgin Annunciate* in Palermo, other than that it is a more complex and mature work than the earlier version in Munich, and is also one of the absolute masterpieces of Italian Quattrocento painting; indeed, it has become an iconic symbol of Antonello's art. Apart from its sophisticated and masterful composition, the work is surprising in its ability to represent, with such a convincing sense of volume and perspective, a type of idealized Mediterranean beauty in an image that is simultaneously abstract and true to life: "[t]hat closed, almost hostile, glance that stereotypical smiles cannot sweeten in the faces of Antonello's Madonnas and Virgins Annunciate, is now sublimated in an expression of noble detachment. Face and gesture render this Virgin intangible in her abstract isolation, enclosed in her blue mantle like a star in the night. The *Virgin Annunciate* of Palermo excludes us from her world with a kind of measured firmness" (Marabottini 1981).

The Madrid *Pietà*, a very late work that was heavily influenced by Bellini, is also one of the most recent additions to Antonello's oeuvre. Several landscape passages (including a fortified city with a church and its ancient bell tower, easily recognizable as the cathedral of Messina) and some areas where the execution is weaker would seem to reveal the hand of an assistant, most likely that of Antonello's son Jacobello, who was busy, documents tell us, after his father's death, finishing the works the master had left incomplete.

Antonello died in Messina probably in February 1479. His first direct followers, including Jacobello (who also died very young, and who proudly signed his works, such as the *Madonna and Child* in the Accademia Carrara, Bergamo, "*filius non humani pictoris*" ["son of the immortal painter"]) and Antonello's nephews Pietro and Antonio de Saliba, strove to imitate the master's pictorial language in works that became ever more pedestrian and repetitive without ever displaying a true understanding of either his originality or his greatness.

The artistic culture of Sicily was also too old-fashioned and too focused on devotional commissions to absorb Antonello's sophisticated language. Other painters active on the island in that period—such as the Siracusan Marco Costanzo; Salvo d'Antonio, another of Antonello's nephews; Antonino Giuffrè; and the rather mediocre Giovanello d'Itala—rehashed formulas and themes derived from Antonello's art throughout the early sixteenth century and beyond, attempting to reconcile them with the emerging taste for the new styles from Umbria, Lazio, and Naples. Yet, not one of these artists can be compared with Antonello—nor would Sicily ever again produce a painter of his genius. Antonello's greatness, magnified, above all, by the impression he had made in Venice, exerted a decisive influence not only on Italian art but subsequently on artistic developments elsewhere in Europe.

THE EXHIBITION

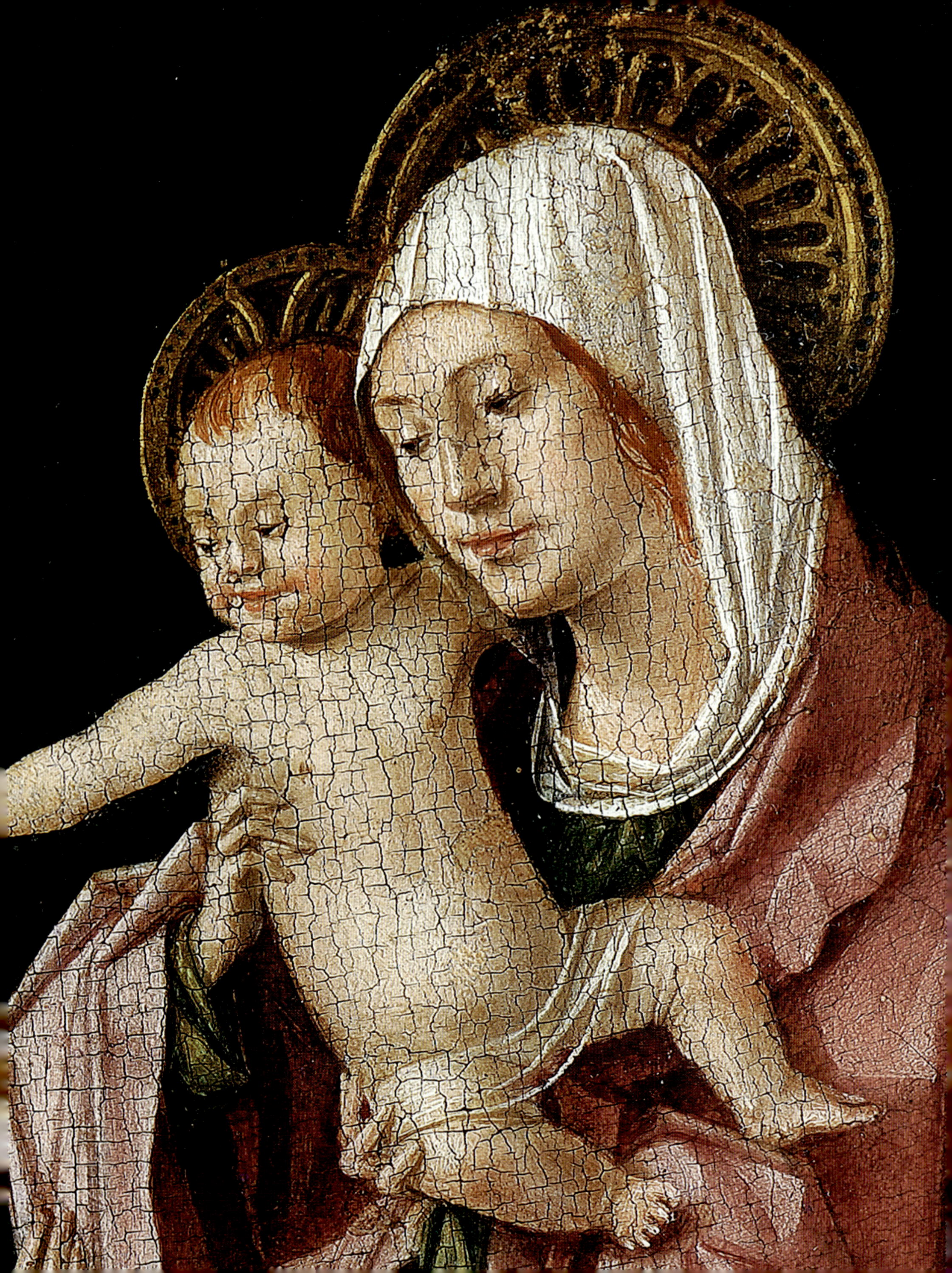

ANTONELLO DA MESSINA

1. *Madonna and Child, with a Praying Franciscan Donor* (recto); *Ecce Homo* (verso)

Oil on panel, 5⅞ × 4¼ in. (15 × 10.7 cm)
Museo Regionale, Messina (inv. 6723)

Only recently rediscovered and attributed to Antonello by Everett Fahy, this small, double-sided portable devotional panel is about the same size as another early two-sided panel (with an *Ecce Homo* on the recto and a *Saint Jerome in the Desert* on the verso) in a private collection in New York (cat. 2). Although subsequent scholarly opinion has been divided on the attribution of this work, since its recent conservation (which has fully restored its legibility) Antonello's authorship seems to be confirmed.

The panel's stylistic characteristics offer numerous analogies with other paintings from Antonello's early period. Closest in style to the *Madonna and Child, with a Praying Franciscan Donor,* are a *Crucifixion* (Muzeul Național de Artă, Bucharest) and the rather later *Annunciation* (Galleria Regionale di Palazzo Bellomo, Siracusa). The figure of Christ in the *Ecce Homo* is more difficult to place stylistically. It is an accomplished work, even though it is much damaged, and the painted framing device, of Catalan inspiration, is a fine invention. As this panel reveals the influence of Netherlandish painting but also exhibits a solid, Renaissance treatment of perspective, it seems likely that it must date no later than the second half of the 1460s.

The panel was acquired at auction by the Messina museum from a private collection in Germany in 2003.

G.B.

Opposite: detail of catalogue 1 (recto)

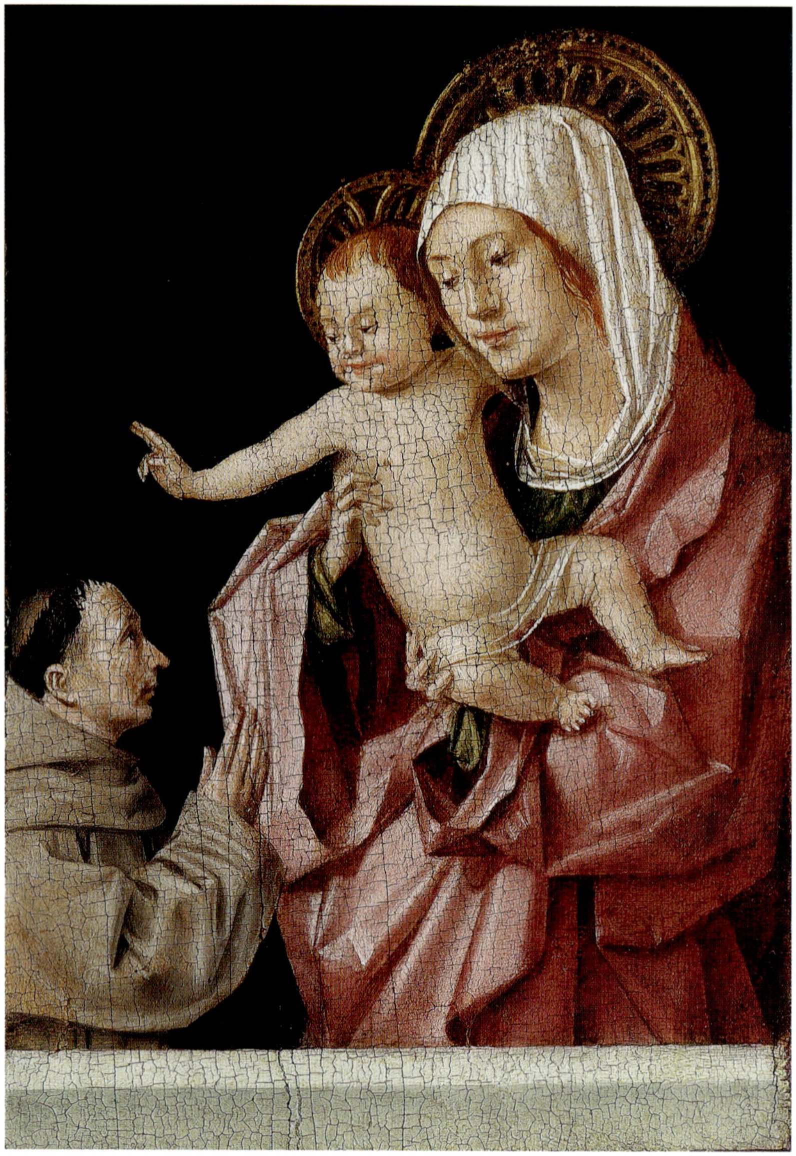

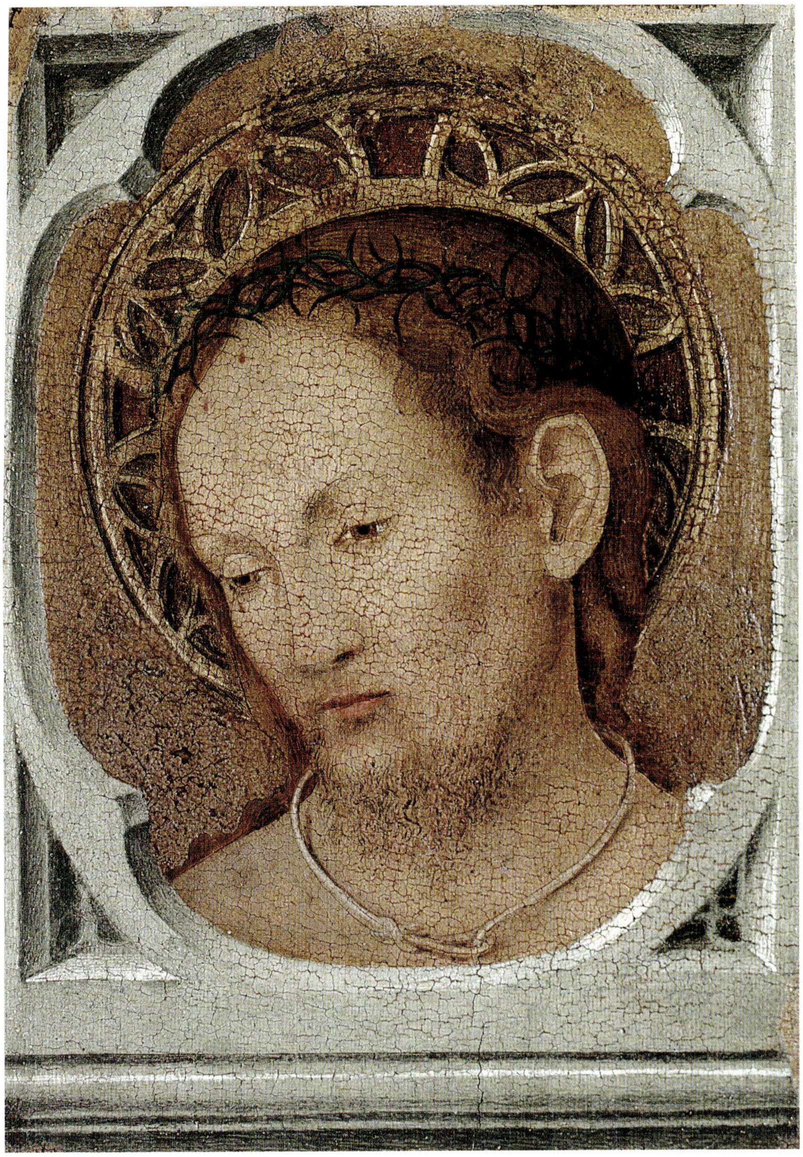

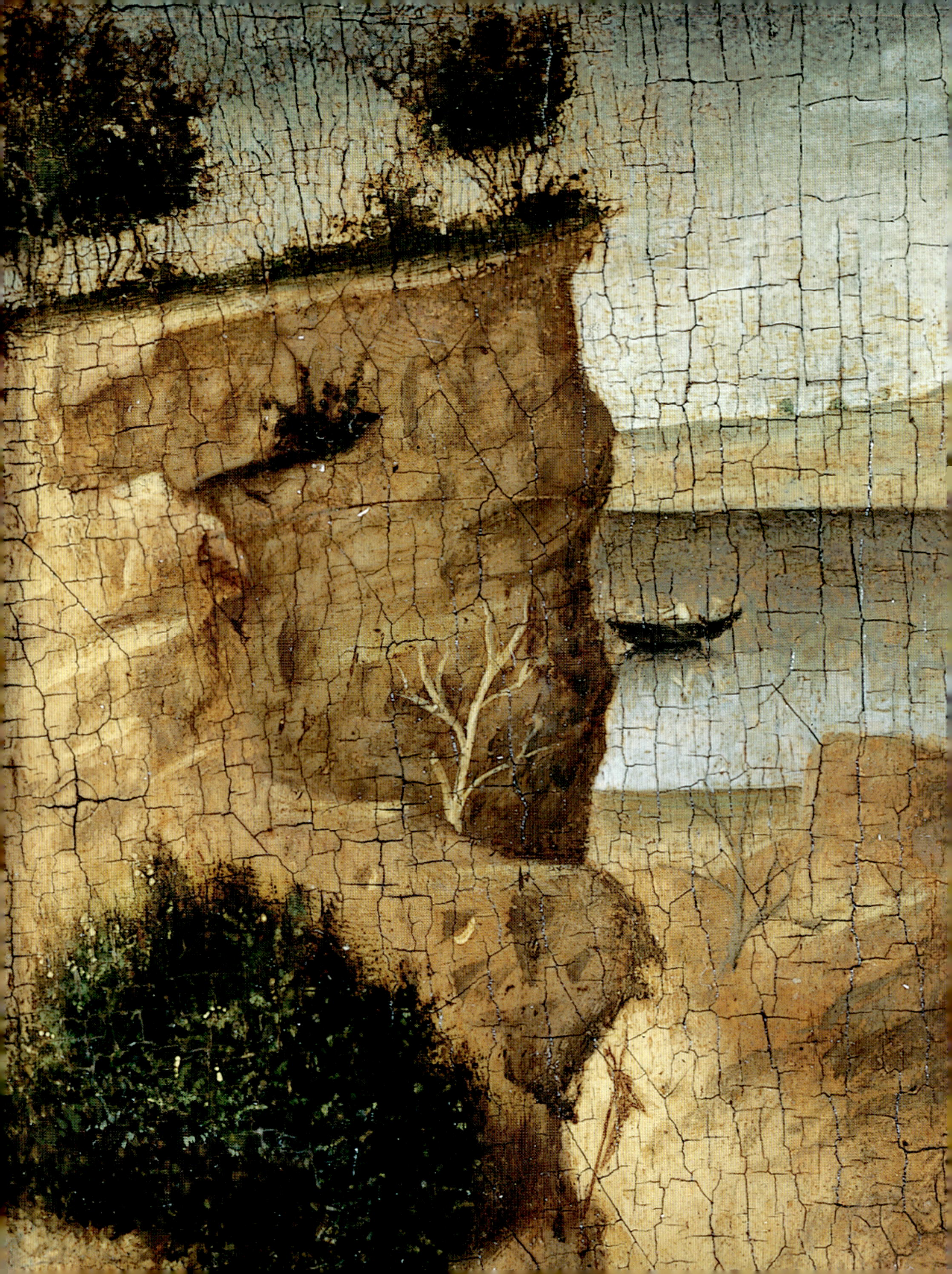

ANTONELLO DA MESSINA

2. *Ecce Homo* (recto); *Saint Jerome in the Desert* (verso)

Oil on panel, 7⅝ × 5½ in. (19.5 × 14 cm)
Private collection

Since the attribution of this tiny panel to Antonello was first proposed by Federico Zeri (1981), and subsequently published by him (1987), it has gained widespread acceptance. Zeri regarded the panel as a kind of precious devotional object that might have been carried in a leather pocketbook and often handled (perhaps accounting for the condition of the figure of Saint Jerome on the reverse). The *Ecce Homo* ("Behold the Man," as declared by Pilate [John 19: 5]) on the recto represents the artist's earliest such treatment of this subject, which engaged his visual imagination and established a popular type of devotional image throughout Northern Italy. Its basic elements have already been worked out here: the bare-chested and bust-length figure of Christ is shown behind a parapet, a crown of thorns encircles his head, and a rope is slipped around his neck. Several features, such as the parapet with the inscription INRI, were influenced by similar details in the Netherlandish paintings that Antonello would have encountered during his early years in Naples.

Both sides of the panel have stylistic connections with other early works by the artist. The marked individuality of Christ's visage finds a parallel in the incisively characterized sitter in the *Portrait of a Man* now in Cefalù (cat. 3)—an interpretation that was repeated in the *Christ Crowned with Thorns* in the Metropolitan Museum (cat. 4). The delicately painted scene on the verso depicts Jerome, his bench, and his books in the midst of a rocky landscape containing bare trees, shrubs, and two snakes. Rugged outcroppings open onto the smooth surface of a lake on which there is a boat, recalling certain works by Jan van Eyck and Petrus Christus. Both the landscape motifs and their disposition echo those in another *Saint Jerome in the Desert* and in the fragmentary *Three Angels Visiting Abraham* (both in the Museo della Magna Grecia, Reggio Calabria). These pictures are usually dated to the early 1460s and demonstrate the ongoing influence of Northern painting on Antonello's work, as well as a new emphasis on spatial construction. While Northern painting was a catalyst for Antonello's imagination, there is no parallel in Netherlandish art for the expressive character of the Christ in the *Ecce Homo*, or for the direct way in which he engages the viewer. This new, empathetic approach to devotional painting prepared the way for his greatest achievements, such as the *Virgin Annunciate* (cat. 6). A.B.

Opposite: detail of catalogue 2 (verso)

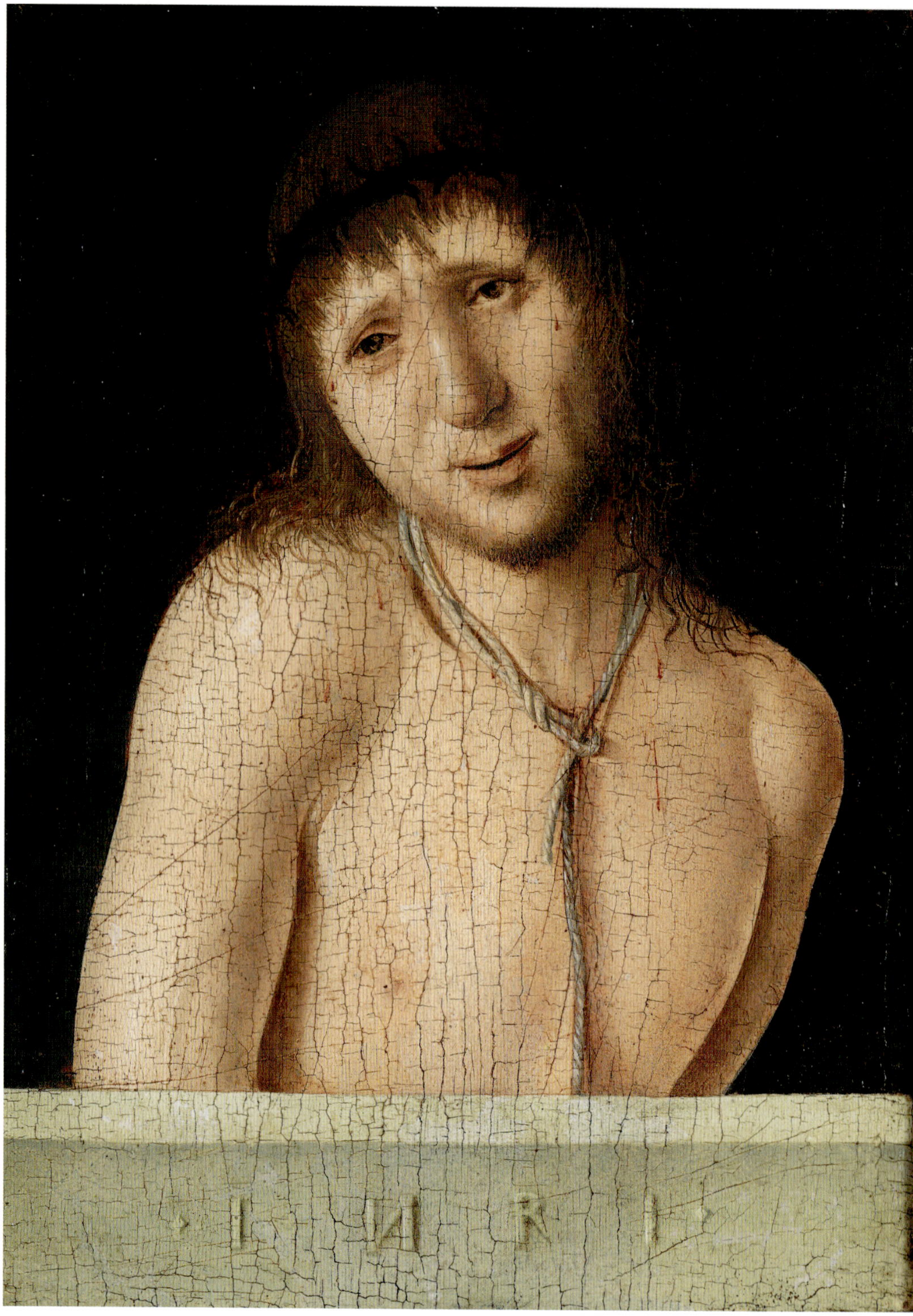
I N R I

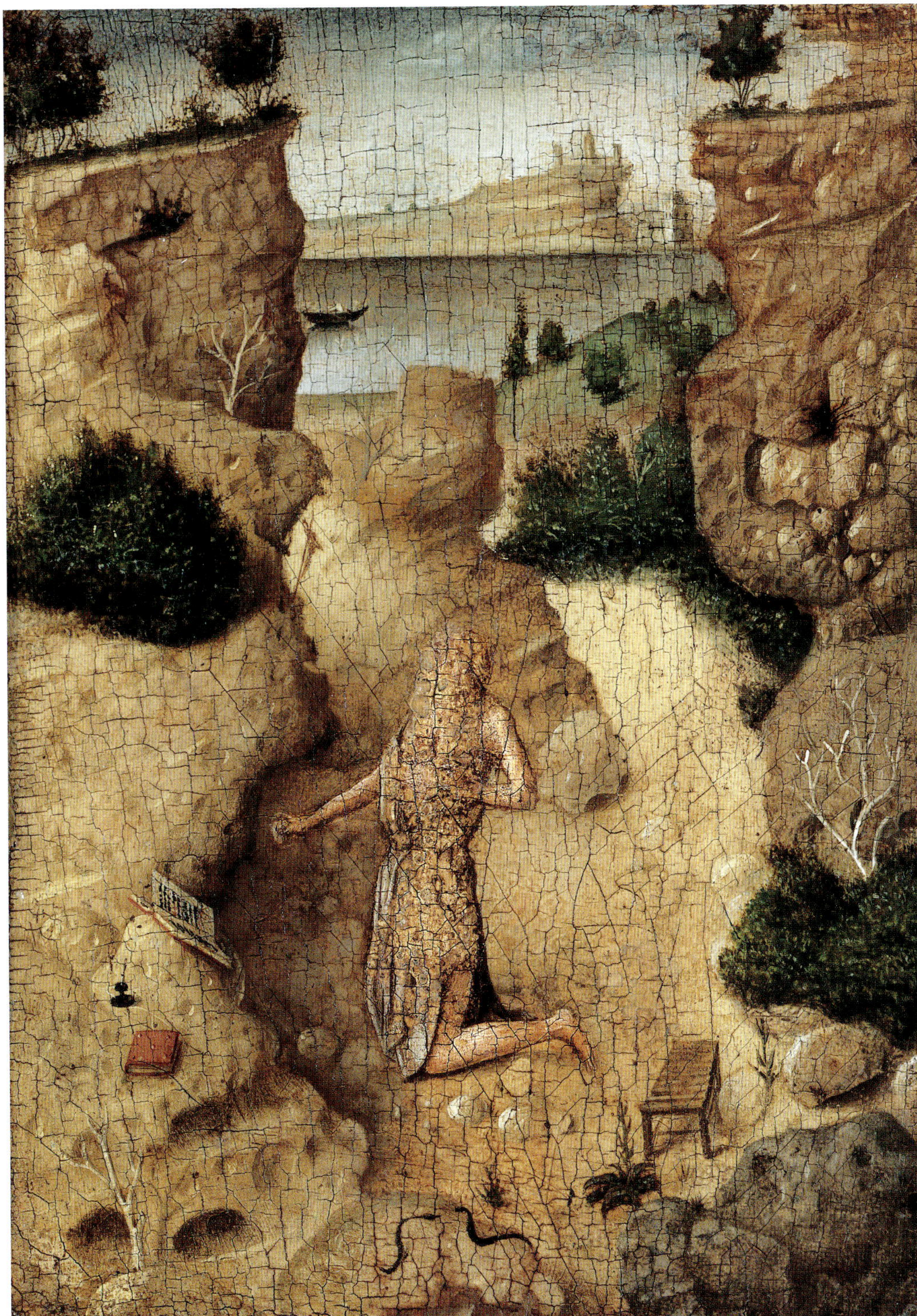

ANTONELLO DA MESSINA

3. *Portrait of a Man*

Oil on panel, 12¼ × 9⅝ in. (31 × 24.5 cm)
Museo della Fondazione Culturale Mandralisca, Cefalù (Palermo)

This early portrait is one of Antonello's best-known works. Traditionally, it is believed to have come from the island of Lipari, where it appears to have been used as the door of a pharmacy cupboard. Baron Enrico Pirajno di Mandralisca acquired the portrait from there, sometime in the nineteenth century, and, with the rest of his collection, it was later donated to the city of Cefalù. A caption in an early-twentieth-century catalogue of photographs identified the work as a portrait of "an unknown sailor," and it retained that evocative title until Roberto Longhi noted (1953), perspicaciously, that "Antonello did not paint portraits of fishermen but of barons (*'baruni'*), even if he also made use of common Sicilian facial features in his religious works."

Scholars have unanimously accepted the attribution of this panel to Antonello, since Di Marzo first proposed it in 1899. The portrait has been plausibly dated to the late 1460s, or perhaps between 1470 and 1472.

G.B.

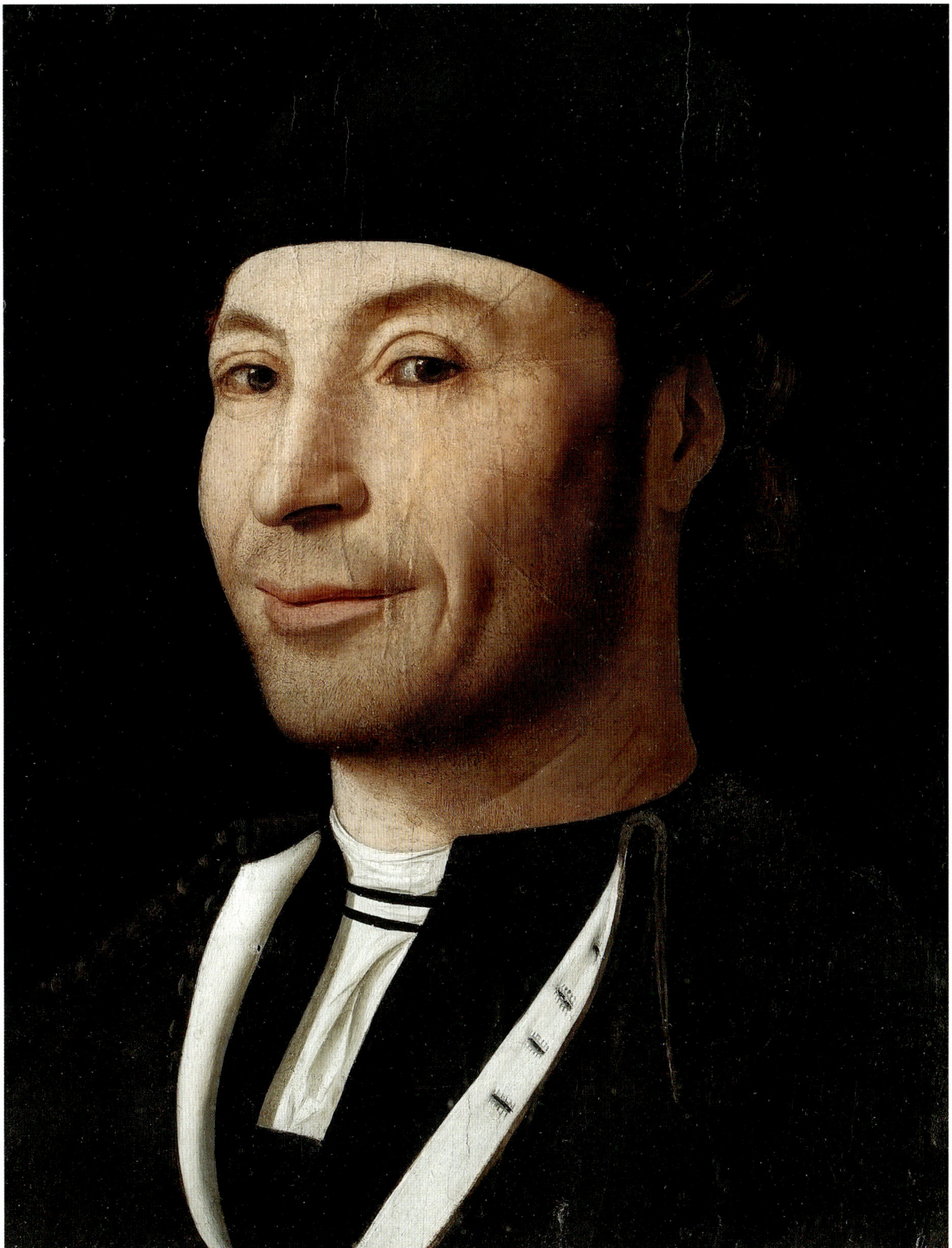

ANTONELLO DA MESSINA

4. *Christ Crowned with Thorns*

Possibly 1470

Oil on panel, 16¾ × 12 in. (42.5 × 30.5 cm)

Signed (lower center): Antonellus messan[us] / me pin[x]it

The Metropolitan Museum of Art, New York. The Friedsam Collection, Bequest of Michael Friedsam, 1931 (32.100.82)

In this moving painting of *Christ Crowned with Thorns,* sometimes called *Ecce Homo,* the artist depicts a bust-length and bare-chested Christ behind a parapet and against a dark background. The downward-cast eyes, the long and rather thick nose, and the slightly parted, full lips evoke both his suffering and his physiognomic individuality without lessening in any way the nobility of his bearing. Antonello returned to this subject repeatedly, giving each variation on the theme slightly different formal characteristics and its own psychological cast. The result was a sublime series of devotional paintings that have been the subject of much recent scholarly attention (Thiébaut; Simonetta).

This picture has been known since the mid-seventeenth century, when it was in the collection of Don Gaspar de Haro y Guzmán, Count-Duke of Olivares (Naples and Palermo), well known as Velázquez's patron. By late in that century it was in Palermo, in the collection of Don Giulio Alliata, and the *cartellino* attached to the parapet was then said to have borne the date 1470, as well as the artist's signature. This seems to have been the date recorded as well by the great connoisseur G. B. Cavalcaselle on the sketch that he made of the painting (the sketchbook is preserved in the Biblioteca Nazionale Marciana, Venice) when he saw it in Naples in 1858. Today the date is illegible, even under infrared reflectography. Nonetheless, 1470 seems a probable date, making this painting slightly later than the *Ecce Homo* in a private collection (cat. 2) but earlier than the example dated 1473 and now in Piacenza (Galleria Alberoni).

The loss of the date is only one aspect of the more widespread abrasion of the picture surface. This is most apparent in the thinly painted shadows and beard, but the flesh tones retain their modeling, as in the highlights down the nose and the subtlety of the rendering of the chest and collarbone. Interestingly, this is one of the few versions of the subject in which Antonello has not included a length of rope knotted around Christ's throat, instead focusing attention on his sorrowful face and beautiful torso, here free of any sign of injury. A.B.

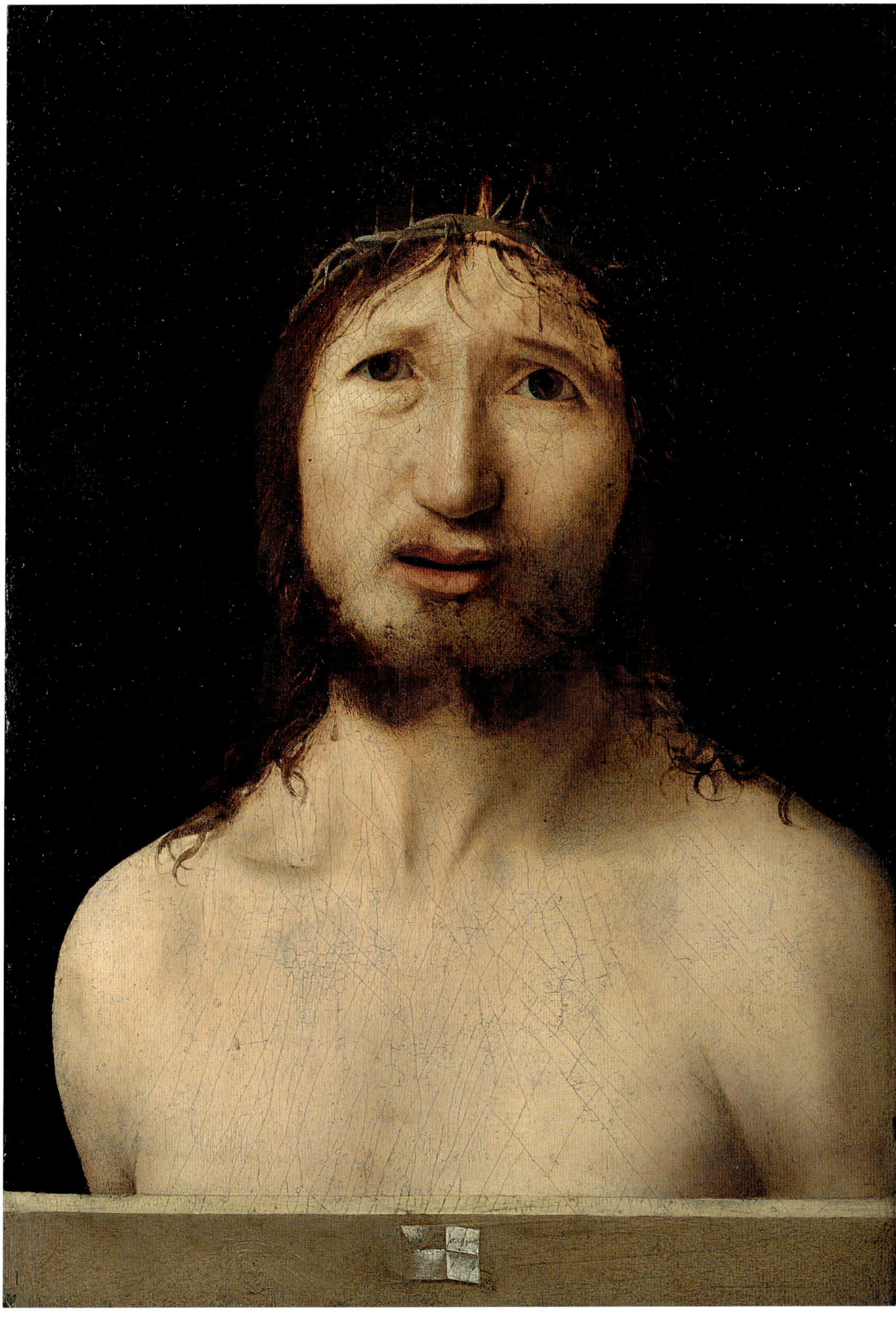

ANTONELLO DA MESSINA

5. *Portrait of a Man*

About 1470

Oil on panel, 10⅝ × 8⅛ in. (27 × 20.6 cm)

The Metropolitan Museum of Art, New York. Bequest of Benjamin Altman, 1913 (14.40.645)

From about 1470 until his death in 1479, Antonello painted one of the most remarkable series of male portraits of the Quattrocento. Deviating from the strict profile poses generally favored by Italian painters and inspired, instead, by Netherlandish portraits, these bust-length images present their sitters in three-quarter view, and almost always against a dark neutral background. This example is among the earliest, painted probably not long after the *Portrait of a Man* in Cefalù (cat. 3). The young man is simply dressed, his dark clothing and long cap setting off the thin white band of his collar and his fine, light, wavy hair (its silhouette against the outline of his face at the left is one of the most virtuosic elements of the painting). His face is animated by the movement of his pale gray eyes, the slight twist of his head, and above all by the hint of a smile—a smile that has been likened to that of a Greek kouros. While Antonello's somewhat later portraits are more monumental and have an even stronger psychological presence, the early ones are rarely surpassed for the charm and vitality of their sitters, or for the sense that they transmit the "motions of the mind," in Leonardo da Vinci's words. Antonello's portraits made a strong impact in Venice, where they may have influenced Giovanni Bellini in the mid-1470s and established the basis for the portraits by Jacometto Veneziano.

Although the surface has been somewhat abraded, especially in the shadows of the flesh tones and in the hair at the right, the panel is generally legible, and the better part of the fine detail and modeling is intact.

A.B.

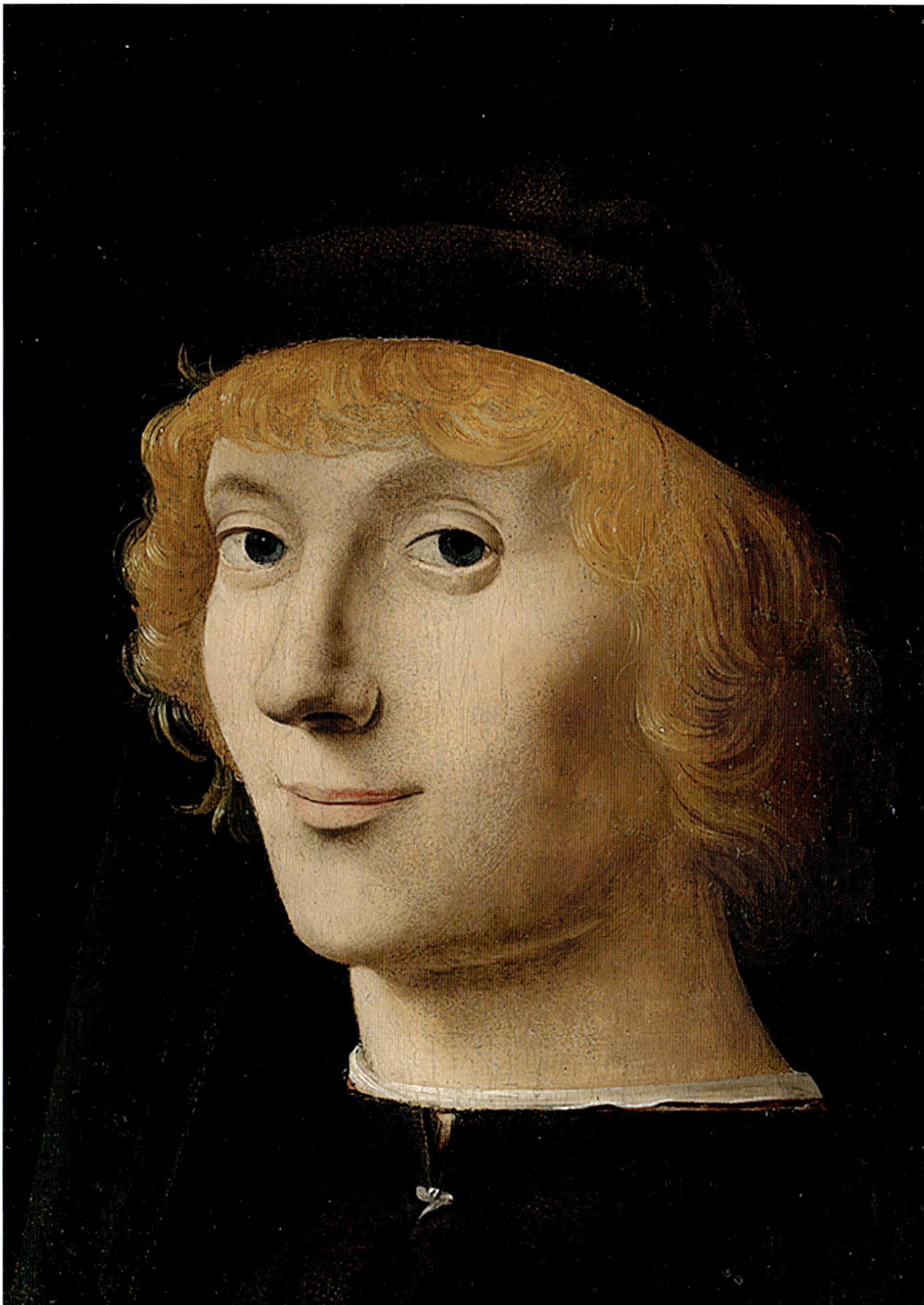

ANTONELLO DA MESSINA

6. *The Virgin Annunciate*

Oil on panel, 17¾ x 13⅝ in. (45 × 34.5 cm)
Galleria Regionale della Sicilia, Palermo (inv. 47)

Although for some time this painting was confused with a rather modest copy in the Galleria dell' Accademia in Venice, it was finally recognized as a masterful addition to Antonello's oeuvre. Since then, its subtle yet magnetic charm has inspired a plethora of differing stylistic and iconographic interpretations. Longhi (1914) declared that the hand "is the most beautiful . . . I have seen in all of painting." The picture's perfect synthesis of formal elements with a masterful handling of space bordering on abstraction has led to universal agreement that the work must date to late in the artist's career—that is, to about 1475–76, at the end of his Venetian sojourn or just following his final return to Messina.

The painting was bequeathed to the Museo Nazionale (later, the Palazzo Abatellis) in 1906 by the Cavaliere Di Giovanni, who had purchased it from the Colluzio family in Palermo as a work by Albrecht Dürer.

G.B.

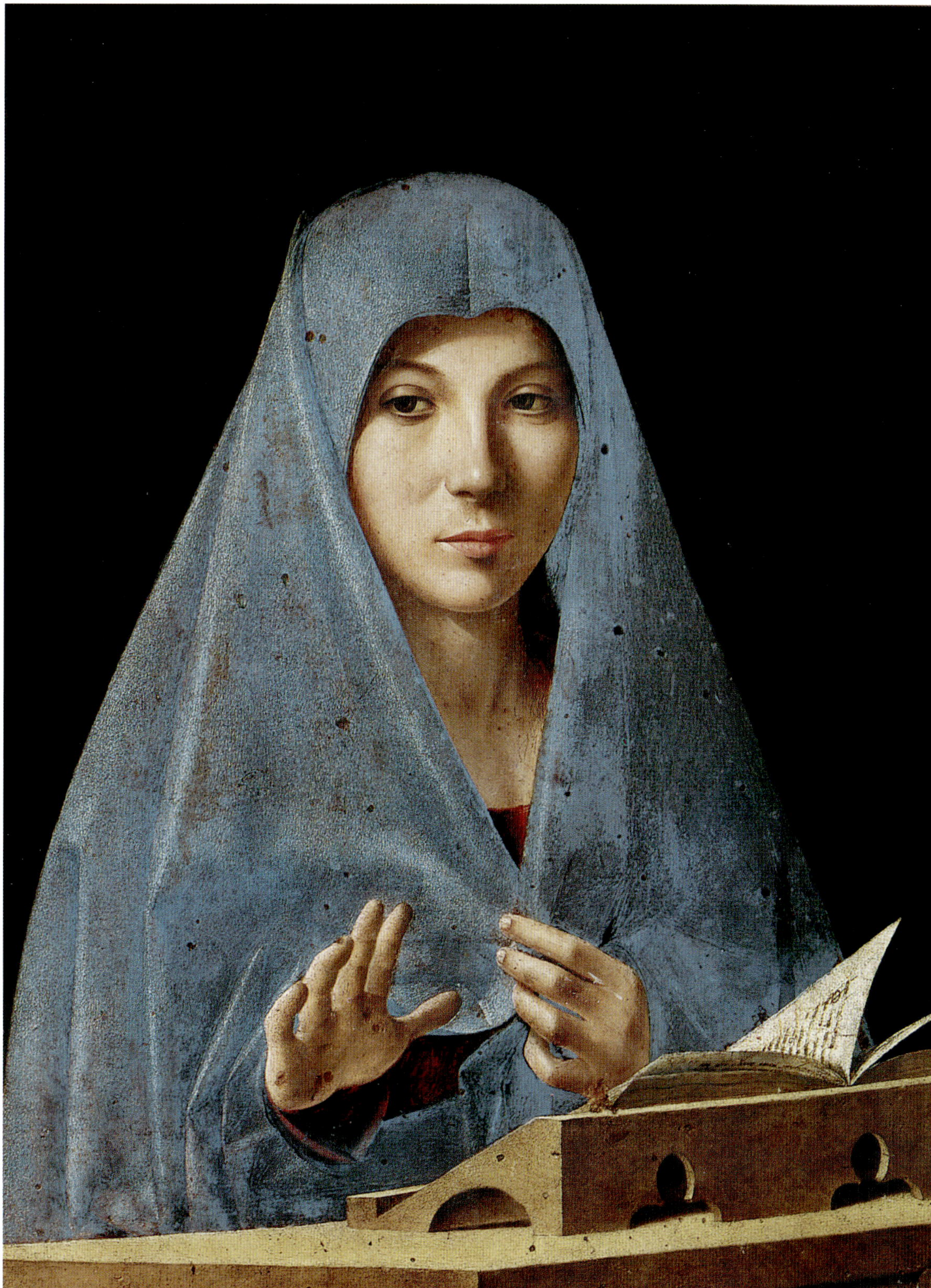

7. *Group of Draped Figures*

Tip of the brush (or fine pen) and brown ink on an irregular sheet, with the upper corners made up, 4⅜ × 5⅞ in. (110 × 149 mm)
The Metropolitan Museum of Art, New York. The Robert Lehman Collection, 1975 (1975.1.265)

Very few drawings can be attributed to Antonello with any certainty. Following Robert Lehman's acquisition of this sheet in the 1920s, it was generally considered a work by the Netherlandish artist Petrus Christus, or by a sculptor in the orbit of Claus Sluter because of the resemblance of its heavily draped figures to the famous *pleurants* (or mourners) on the latter's tomb sculptures in Dijon. The alternative attribution to Antonello da Messina was made independently by Julius Held (letter of 1938) and Roberto Longhi (1953). It was Longhi who associated the study with the group of "Burgundian" mourners at the foot of the cross in Antonello's early *Crucifixion* (Muzeul Național de Artă, Bucharest), a painting probably dating from the 1460s; this suggestion was rather widely accepted. The interpretation of the drawing became more complex when, in 1983, the Louvre acquired a closely related sheet. The bottom half includes six identical women, with an additional four at the right side. Above the women on the Louvre sheet, however, rises a majestic series of buildings shown in deep perspective. Tall crenellated palaces and towers recede in space to an arched gate, before which is a tiny figure. The tunneling perspective is reminiscent of that in drawings from Jacopo Bellini's sketchbooks, and there is nothing quite like it in Antonello's work before his Venetian period—more specifically, until the background of the *Saint Sebastian* painted for the church of San Giuliano in Venice (fig. 2), perhaps as late as 1478 (Lucco 1990). This raises the possibility that both drawings date from the later 1470s, although the connection of the figures to somewhat earlier Burgundian and Netherlandish art cannot be denied. It also remains an open question as to whether both drawings are autograph works by the master. Anna Forlani Tempesti and Dominique Thiébaut have noted (1991, 1993) that the Lehman sheet is not as precise and delicate in its details, or as convincingly descriptive (although drawn in a distinctive, stippled technique). Thus, our drawing may be a less carefully executed autograph replica, or one produced in the artist's workshop following his design.

A.B.

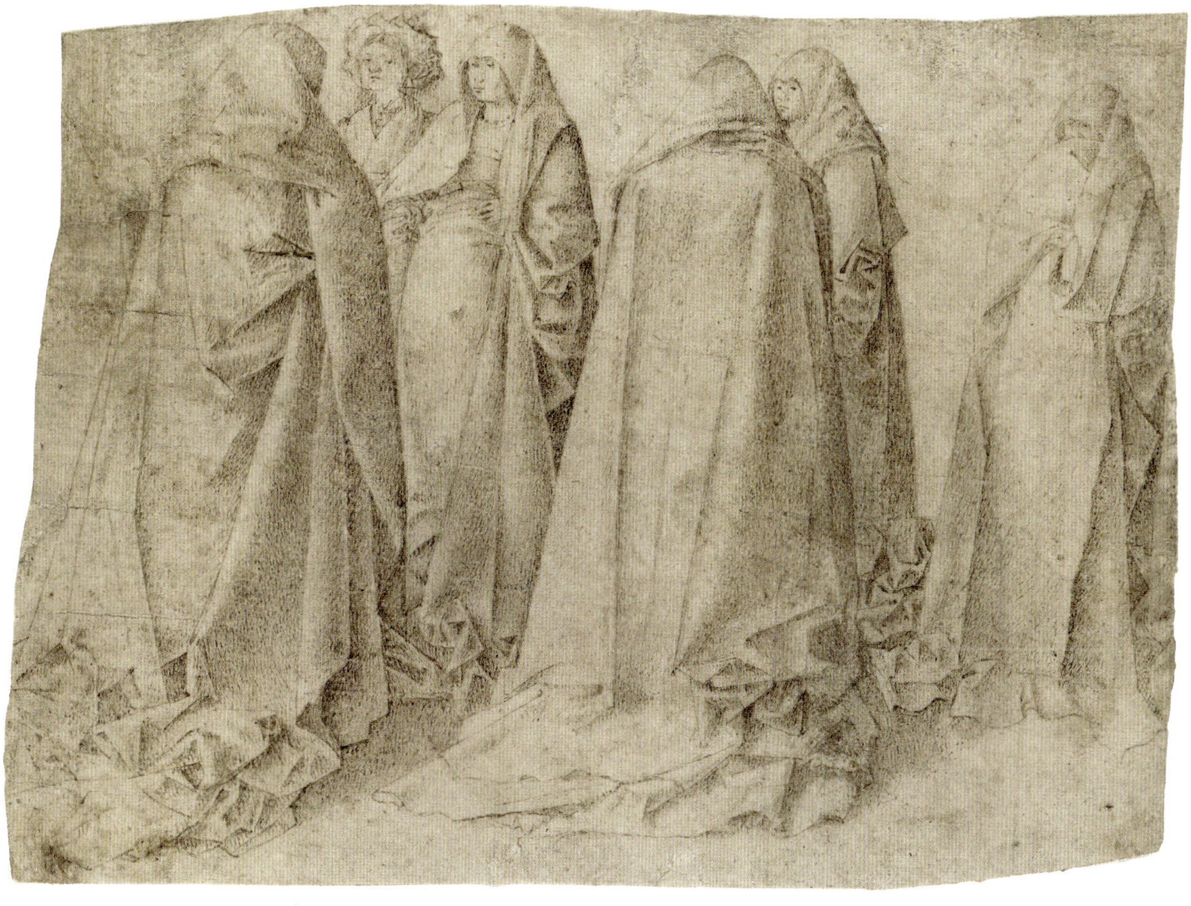

Checklist of Other Exhibited Works

Attributed to Barthélemy d'Eyck
Netherlandish (active 1444–69)

Famous Men and Women from Classical and Biblical Antiquity

Pen and brown ink, and brush and watercolor of various hues, with traces of gold paint, on vellum, 12 3/16 × 7 7/8 in. (310 × 200 mm)
The Metropolitan Museum of Art, New York. Bequest of Walter C. Baker, 1971 (1972.118.10)

Petrus Christus
Netherlandish (active by 1444–died 1475/76)

Head of Christ

Oil on parchment, laid down on panel: parchment, 5 3/4 × 4 1/8 in. (14.6 × 10.5 cm)
The Metropolitan Museum of Art, New York. Bequest of Lillian S. Timken, 1959 (60.71.1)

Petrus Christus
Netherlandish (active by 1444–died 1475/76)

The Lamentation

Oil on panel: painted surface, 10 × 13 3/4 in. (25.4 × 34.9 cm)
The Metropolitan Museum of Art, New York. Marquand Collection, Gift of Henry G. Marquand, 1890 (91.26.12)

Jacometto (Jacometto Veneziano)
Italian, Venetian (active about 1472–died before 1498)

Portrait of a Young Man

Oil on panel, 11 × 8 1/4 in. (27.9 × 21 cm)
The Metropolitan Museum of Art, New York. The Jules Bache Collection, 1949 (49.7.3)

Biographical Note

Antonello di Giovanni d'Antonio was born in Messina, presumably between 1425 and 1430, to Giovanni d'Antonio, a "*magister mazonus*" (a stone- or marble cutter), and his wife, Garita (Margherita ?). Both the early Southern Italian sources and Giorgio Vasari's biography of the artist offer confusing and sometimes dubious information about Antonello's life, with the latter claiming that he traveled to the Netherlands, where he met Jan van Eyck, an event that is chronologically impossible. It is only because of the research of the Sicilian scholars Gioacchino Di Marzo and Gaetano La Corte Cailler, at the turn of the twentieth century, that we have the framework of a biography of the artist and a preliminary catalogue of his oeuvre; their scholarship provided a starting point for all later students of Antonello's career.

All early suggestions that the young Antonello journeyed to Palermo or even to Lombardy were laid to rest by the famous letter the humanist Pietro Summonte wrote to the Venetian Marcantonio Michiel in 1524 (published in Nicolini 1925). The letter makes it clear that Antonello apprenticed in the workshop of Niccolò Colantonio in Naples sometime between 1445 and 1455, at a time when that city was very much open to Netherlandish as well as Spanish and Provençal artistic influences. Antonello was already an independent master in March 1457 when he was commissioned to paint a processional standard for the confraternity of San Michele dei Gerbini in Reggio Calabria similar to one he had already executed for the confraternity of San Michele in Messina (both are now lost). He was the head of a thriving workshop in which his brother Giordano and Paolo di Ciacio worked as apprentices. Scholars have also suggested that it was during this period, and certainly before 1460, that Antonello made a trip to Rome, where he would have seen the works of Fra Angelico and Piero della Francesca.

Numerous archival documents from 1460, when Antonello's father, Giovanni, hired a boat to bring his son "magister Antonellus" and his family home to Messina from Amantea in Calabria, confirm Antonello's presence in his native city, up until 1465. The majority of this documentation is related to commissions for works of art that are now lost. On January 30, 1461, he and another Messinese artist, Giovanni Mirulla, were asked to make an image of the "glorious Virgin Mary" and to deliver it by the end of Lent; on July 5, 1462, he was commissioned to paint a standard for the confraternity of Sant'Elia dei Disciplinati identical to others he had made for the confraternities of Santa Maria della Carità and of San Michele. In 1463 he had already executed "*quondam iconam*" (several images) for the confraternity of San Nicolò alla Montagna.

A hiatus in the documents between July 1465 and October 1471 has led scholars to propose that Antonello traveled again to the mainland, where he would have had another opportunity to see the works of Piero della Francesca; this hypothesis is supported by the stylistic direction his work took after 1470. Archival sources from 1471 to 1474 record that Antonello was again very active in Messina and eastern Sicily. Three recently discovered notarial acts, dated October 21, 1471, and January 15 and June 22, 1472, attest to the artist's presence in the Sicilian city of Noto, where he executed a (now lost) standard for the confraternity of the Holy Spirit. The following year he was commissioned to paint a large polyptych for the church of San Giacomo in Caltagirone and a standard for the confraternity of the Holy Trinity in Randazzo (both, now lost).

Antonello was in Venice in late 1475 and early 1476, his presence there documented in a letter that the humanist Matteo Colazio wrote to Antonio degli Adimari in 1475 in which Antonello is mentioned as busy painting the San Cassiano altarpiece. This information is confirmed by another letter that Pietro Bon, who commissioned that altarpiece, sent to Galeazzo Maria Sforza, Duke of Milan, on March 16, 1476, begging the duke to allow Antonello to finish the nearly completed work before summoning him to

Milan to be his court portraitist. Bon claimed that once it was finished the altarpiece would be "one of the most excellent painted works either in or outside of Italy."

Possibly following a very brief stay in Milan, by as early as September 1476 Antonello had returned to Messina, where he would remain for the rest of his life. In September 1476 he made the last payment on the dowry for his daughter Caterinella, as stipulated in the contract with his son-in-law, Bernardo Casalaina, of 1473. On June 20, 1477, Antonello and his brother-in-law, the wood-carver Giovanni di Saliba, were commissioned to make a standard (now lost) for the Church of the Annunziata in Ficarra (in the province of Messina), and that same year he was paid for several services or works (*beneficii*) he carried out for the cathedral of Catania (*maiuri ecclesia*). On November 5, 1478, Ruggero De Luca of Randazzo commissioned Antonello to make a banner with an "image of the most sacred Virgin Mary with her Son in her arms and surrounded by four angels." This work, left unfinished at the artist's death, was completed by his son Jacobello—who had inherited his father's workshop—along with a painting for the confraternity of the church of Santa Maria della Carità and a standard for San Michele in Catania (Jacobello was still working on the standard in 1480). The exact date of Antonello's death is not known, although it certainly occurred between February 14, 1479, when "lying ill in bed" he dictated his last will, and May 11 of that same year, when his testament was opened and read. G.B.

Participating Museums in Sicily

Cefalù, Museo della Fondazione Culturale Mandralisca
Founded in 1866, the museum's rich collections comprise archaeological, numismatic, and art objects, and artifacts of natural history, which were donated to the city by Baron Enrico Pirajno di Mandralisca (1809–1864). In addition to the Pinacoteca, its most notable holdings are a red-figure krater of the fourth century B.C. depicting a tuna seller, and the numismatic and malacological collections. The famous *Portrait of a Man* by Antonello da Messina will soon be newly installed through the efforts of the Centro Regionale per la Progettazione e il Restauro.

Messina, Museo Regionale
The museum is situated on the coast to the north of the city, near the Annunziata River. The late-nineteenth-century building was formerly the Barbera-Mellinghoff spinning mill; following the devastating earthquake of 1908, it was designated as the new museum, and opened to the public in 1922. Over the course of the following years (most recently in 1984) the building has undergone several renovations with the overall goal of improving the conditions in which the art is exhibited.

The museum highlights the city's artistic culture of the twelfth through the eighteenth centuries, emphasizing such local personalities as the artists Antonello da Messina and Girolamo Alibrando; the painters Polidoro da Caravaggio and Michelangelo Merisi, known as Caravaggio, who spent time in Sicily; and the sculptor Giovanni Angelo Montorsoli. After the 1908 earthquake, paintings, sculpture, and precious decorative objects rescued from destroyed buildings were added to the nucleus of the collections of the Museo Civico.

The museum will soon be expanded, as a large complex of buildings near the current structure is about to be completed.

Palermo, Galleria Regionale della Sicilia, Palazzo Abatellis
The Galleria Regionale is situated in the historic center of the city in the via Alloro, the principal artery of the old quarter called the Kalsa. The building, the work of the Sicilian architect Matteo Carnalivari, was completed at the end of the fifteenth century, and was the home of Francesco Abatellis—"Maestro Portulano del Regno" (Harbormaster of the Kingdom); it is one of the most architecturally noteworthy palaces in western Sicily in the Gothic–Catalan style. Later, the palace was converted into a monastery and was variously modified over time. Gravely damaged by the bombardment of 1943, it was restored in 1953–54, and, with a collection impressively installed by Carlo Scarpa, it became the Galleria Nazionale (now Regionale) of Sicily.

The Galleria Regionale documents the evolution of western Sicily's artistic culture of the twelfth through the eighteenth centuries, its holdings comprising acquisitions, gifts, and the transferral of works of art from religious organizations following their suppression. Before their current installation in the Galleria Regionale, these works were part of the Pinacoteca della Regia Università and then, from 1866, the Museo Nazionale di Palermo.

On the ground floor the visitor encounters sculpture from the twelfth through the sixteenth centuries, including the bust of *Eleanora d'Aragona* by Francesco Laurana and the great fifteenth-century fresco of *The Triumph of Death*. The first floor is home to the Pinacoteca, with a collection ranging from various monumental fifteenth-century crucifixes and the Malvagna triptych by Jan Gossaert, called Mabuse, to works by artists active in Southern Italy, such as Vincenzo da Pavia, Pietro Novelli, Mattia Preti, and Francesco Solimena.

Selected Bibliography

ANTONELLO DA MESSINA

PRIMARY SOURCES

Fausto Nicolini. *L'arte napoletana del Rinascimento e la lettera di Pietro Summonte a Marco Antonio Michiel* [1524], pp. 160–62, 210–14. Naples, 1925.

Giorgio Vasari. *Le vite de' più eccellenti architetti, pittori et scultori italiani da Cimabue insino a' tempi nostri* [1550 ed.], edited by Luciano Bellosi and Aldo Rossi. Turin, 1986.

Giorgio Vasari. *Le vite de' più eccellenti pittori, scultori e architettori* [1568 ed.], edited by Paola Della Pergola, Luigi Grassi, and Giovanni Previtali. Novara, 1967.

Francesco Susinno. *Le vite de' pittori messinesi* [ms. ca. 1724], edited by Valentino Martinelli, pp. 17–29. Florence, 1960.

Gioacchino Di Marzo and Gaetano La Corte Cailler. *Scritti su Antonello da Messina,* edited by A. Borda Bossana; introduction by G. Molonia. Messina, 1999.

MONOGRAPHS AND EXHIBITION CATALOGUES

Gioacchino Di Marzo. *Di Antonello da Messina e dei suoi congiunti: Studi e documenti.* Documenti per servire alla storia di Sicilia, 9. Palermo, 1903. Reprinted, Palermo, 1983.

Jan Lauts. *Antonello da Messina.* Vienna, 1940.

Stefano Bottari. *Antonello.* Milan and Messina, 1953.

Giorgio Vigni and Giovanni Carandente, eds. *Antonello da Messina e la pittura del Quattrocento in Sicilia.* Exhib. cat., Palazzo Comunale di Messina. Venice, 1953.

Raffaello Causa. *Antonello da Messina.* I maestri del colore, 23. Milan, 1964.

Gabriele Mandel. *L'opera completa di Antonello da Messina.* Introduction by Leonardo Sciascia. Milan, 1967.

Alessandro Marabottini and Fiorella Sricchia Santoro, eds. *Antonello da Messina.* Exhib. cat., Museo Regionale, Messina. Rome, 1981.

Eugenio Battisti. *Antonello: Il teatro sacro, gli spazi, la donna.* Il labirinto, 7. Palermo, 1985. 2nd ed., Palermo, 1993.

Fiorella Sricchia Santoro. *Antonello e l'Europa.* Milan, 1986.

Antonello da Messina: Atti del Convegno di Studi tenuto a Messina, dal 29 novembre al 2 dicembre 1981. Messina: Università degli Studi di Messina, Facoltà di Lettere e Filosofia, 1987.

Gioacchino Barbera, ed. *Il restauro dell'Annunciazione di Antonello da Messina.* Exhib. cat., Museo Regionale di Palazzo Bellomo, Siracusa. Siracusa, 1987.

Luciana Arbace. *Antonello da Messina: Catalogo completo dei dipinti.* I gigli dell'arte, 29. Florence, 1993.

Dominique Thiébaut. *Le Christ à la colonne d'Antonello de Messine.* Exhib. cat., Musée du Louvre, Paris. Paris, 1993.

Gioacchino Barbera. *Antonello da Messina.* Milan, 1998.

Chiara Savettieri. *Antonello da Messina.* Palermo, 1998.

Farida Simonetti, ed. *Ecce Homo: Antonello da Messina. Genova e Piacenza, due versioni a confronto: Atti della giornata internazionale di studi.* Genoa, 2000.

Cristina Acidini and Antonio Paolucci, eds. *Antonello agli Uffizi: Un acquisto dello Stato per il riscatto dell'eredità Bardini.* Exhib. cat., Piazzale degli Uffizi, Florence. Florence, 2002.

Paolo Biscottini, ed. *Antonello da Messina: Ecce homo.* Exhib. cat., Museo Diocesano, Milan. Milan, 2002.

Lionello Puppi. *Antonello da Messina: San Girolamo nello studio.* Milan, 2003.

PERIODICAL ARTICLES AND ESSAYS

Gaetano La Corte Cailler. "Antonello da Messina: Studi e ricerche con documenti inedite." *Archivio storico messinese* 4 (1903), pp. 332–441.

Roberto Longhi. "Frammento siciliano." *Paragone* 4, no. 47 (1953), pp. 3–44. Reprinted in Roberto Longhi, *Opere complete,* vol. 8, no. 1. Florence, 1975.

Federico Zeri. "Un riflesso di Antonello da Messina a Firenze." *Paragone* 9, no. 99 (1958), pp. 16–21.

Maria Grazia Paolini. "Antonello e la sua scuola." In *Storia della Sicilia,* vol. 5, pp. 273–333. Naples, 1979.

Giovanni Previtali. "Da Antonello da Messina a Jacopo di Antonello," part 1, "La data del 'Cristo benedicente' della National Gallery di Londra"; part 2, "Il 'Cristo deposto' del Museo del Prado." *Prospettiva,* nos. 20–21 (1980), pp. 27–34, 45–57.

Lionello Puppi. "Il viaggio ed il soggiorno a Venezia di Antonello da Messina." *Museum Patavinum* 1, no. 2 (1983), pp. 253–82.

Lionello Puppi. "Un racconto di morte e di immortalità: 'San Girolamo nello studio' di Antonello da Messina." In *Modi del raccontare,* edited by Giulio Ferroni, pp. 34–45. Palermo, 1987.

Fiorella Sricchia Santoro. "De Antonio, Antonello (Antonello da Messina)." In *Dizionario biografico degli Italiani,* vol. 33, pp. 309–15. Rome, 1987.

Federico Zeri. "Prima conversazione." In *Dietro l'Immagine,* pp. 7–36. Milan, 1987.

Mauro Lucco. "Venezia." In *Il Quattrocento: La pittura nel Veneto,* vol. 2, pp. 395–480, esp. p. 484. Milan, 1990.

Anna Forlani Tempesti. Entry (*Group of Draped Figures,* The Metropolitan Museum of Art, New York). In *The Robert Lehman Collection, V: Italian Fifteenth- to Seventeenth-Century Drawings,* by Anna Forlani Tempesti, pp. 182–85. New York, 1991.

Gioacchino Barbera. "Visione fiamminga e misura rinascimentale italiana nella pittura di Antonello da Messina." In *Grandi Siciliani: Tre millenni di civiltà,* vol. 1, pp. 115–20. Catania, 1992.

Rosanna De Gennaro. "Cavalcaselle in Sicilia: Alla ricerca di Antonello da Messina." *Prospettiva,* no. 68 (October 1992), pp. 73–86.

R. Goffen. Entry (*Pietà,* Museo Correr, Venice). In *Carpaccio, Bellini, Tura, Antonello e altri restauri quattrocenteschi della Pinacoteca del Museo Correr,* edited by Attilia Dorigato, pp. 66–69, 162–72. Exhib. cat., Museo Correr, Venice. Milan, 1993.

Joanne Wright. "Antonello in Formazione: Un riesame della 'Crocifissione' di Bucarest." *Arte Veneta* 45 (1993), pp. 20–31.

Federico Zeri. "Premessa ad un Antonello"; and Maria Teresa Fiorio. "Antonello perduto, Antonello ritrovato." In *Antonella da Messina: Un capolavoro per la Pinacoteca del Castello Sforzesco.* Milan, 1995.

Grigore Arbore Popescu. Entry (*Crocifissione,* Muzeul Național de Artă, Bucharest). In *Da Antonello da Messina a Rembrandt: Capolavori d'arte europea dal Museo Nazionale d'Arte di Romania, Bucarest, e dal Museo Nazionale di Brukenthal, Sibiu,* edited by Grigore Arbore Popescu, pp. 22–25. Exhib. cat., Museo della Permanente, Milan. Milan, 1996.

E. Rossetti Brezzi. Entry (*Ritratto d'uomo,* Museo Civico d'Arte Antica, Turin). In *Il tesoro della città: Opere d'arte e oggetti preziosi da Palazzo Madama,* edited by Silvana Pettenati and Giovanni Romano, p. 195. Exhib. cat., Palazzina di Caccia di Stupinigi, Turin. Turin, 1996.

Maria Teresa Fiorio. Entry (*San Benedetto,* Pinacoteca del Castello Sforzesco, Milan). In *Museo d'Arte Antica del Castello Sforzesco: Pinacoteca,* edited by Maria Teresa Fiorio, vol. 1, pp. 104–7. Milan, 1997.

Bernard Aikema. Entry (*San Girolamo nello studio,* National Gallery, London). In *Il Rinascimento a Venezia e la pittura del Nord ai tempi di Bellini, Dürer, Tiziano,* edited by Bernard Aikema, Beverly Louise Brown, Giovanna Nepi Sciré, pp. 214–17. Exhib. cat., Palazzo Grassi, Venice. Milan, 1999.

Fiorella Sricchia Santoro. "Il 'San Girolamo nello studio' di Antonello da Messina." In *Antonello a Napoli,* pp. 5–12. Exhib. cat., Museo e Gallerie Nazionale di Capodimonte, Naples. Naples, 2001.

Enrica Pagella. Entry (*Ritratto d'uomo,* Museo Civico d'Arte Antica, Turin). In *Van Eyck, Antonello, Leonardo: Tre capolavori del Rinascimento,* edited by Giovanna Giacobello Bernard and Enrica Pagella, pp. 12–13. Exhib. cat., Biblioteca Reale, Turin. Turin, 2003.

GENERAL STUDIES

MESSINA AND SICILY IN THE 15TH CENTURY

Stefano Bottari. *La pittura del Quattrocento in Sicilia.* Messina and Florence, 1954.

Salvatore Tramontana. *Antonello e la sua città.* Palermo, 1981. 2nd ed., Palermo, 1999.

F. Campagna Cicala. "La pittura in Sicilia nel Quattrocento." In *La pittura in Italia: Il Quattrocento,* edited by Federico Zeri, vol. 2, pp. 478–87. Milan, 1989.

Teresa Pugliatti. *Pittura del Cinquecento in Sicilia: La Sicilia orientale,* pp. 14–67. Naples, 1993.

Giuseppe Miligi, ed. *Francescanesimo al femminile: Chiara d'Assisi ed Eustochia da Messina.* Messina e la sua storia, 11. Messina, 1994.

Pierluigi Leone De Castris, ed. *Quattrocento aragonese: La pittura a Napoli al tempo di Alfonso e Ferrante d'Aragona.* Exhib. cat., Castel Nuovo, Naples. Naples, 1997.

Ferdinando Bologna, ed. *Il polittico di Colantonio a San Lorenzo.* Exhib. cat., Museo e Gallerie Nazionale di Capodimonte, Naples. Naples, 2001.

ITALY AND THE NORTH IN THE 15TH CENTURY AND THE MEDITERRANEAN RENAISSANCE

Ferdinando Bologna. *Napoli e le rotte mediterranee della pittura: Da Alfonso il Magnanimo a Ferdinando il Cattolico.* Naples, 1977.

Liana Castelfranchi Vegas. *Italia e Fiandra nella pittura del Quattrocento.* Milan, 1983.

Mauro Natale, ed. *El Renacimiento mediterráneo: Viajes de artistas y itinerarios de obras entre Italia, Francia y España en el siglo XV.* Exhib. cat., Museo Thyssen-Bornemisza, Madrid; Museo de Bellas Artes, Valencia. Madrid, 2001.

Till-Holger Borchert, ed. *The Age of Van Eyck: The Mediterranean World and Early Netherlandish Painting, 1430–1530.* Exhib. cat., Groeningemuseum, Bruges. Ghent and Amsterdam, 2002.

Photograph Credits

All photographs are courtesy of the lenders, except for the following:

Alinari / Art Resource, New York: Figure 1

Erich Lessing / Art Resource, New York: Figure 2, 3

Scala / Art Resource, New York: Figure 4